30th KI Workshop on Planen, Scheduling und Konfigurieren, Entwerfen 2016

Klagenfurt, Austria
26 September 2016

ISBN: 978-1-5108-3209-1

Printed from e-media with permission by:

Curran Associates, Inc.
57 Morehouse Lane
Red Hook, NY 12571

Some format issues inherent in the e-media version may also appear in this print version.

Printed by Curran Associates, Inc. (2017)

For permission requests, please contact Universität Oldenburg
at the address below.

Universität Oldenburg
Ammerlander Heerstraße 114-118
D-26129 Oldenburg
Germany

Phone: +49-441-798-0
Fax: +49-441-798-3000

www.uni-oldenburg.de/en

Additional copies of this publication are available from:

Curran Associates, Inc.
57 Morehouse Lane
Red Hook, NY 12571 USA
Phone: 845-758-0400
Fax: 845-758-2633
Email: curran@proceedings.com
Web: www.proceedings.com

TABLE OF CONTENTS

Using AI Planning Techniques in OpenCCG: Detecting Infeasible Composites in Sentence Generation 1
Maximilian Schwenger, Alvaro Torralba, Jorg Hoffmann, David Howcroft, Vera Demberg

Automated Data Management Workflow Generation with Ontologies and Planning 14
N/A

Transforming Complex Business Challenges into Opportunities for Innovative Change - An Application for Planning and Scheduling Technology 27
Brian Drabble, Bernd Schattenberg

Declarative Decomposition and Dispatching for Large-Scale Job-Shop Scheduling 34
Giacomo Da Col and Erich C. Teppan

Scheduling Regarding Energy Efficiency 48
Jürgen Sauer

Author Index

Using AI Planning Techniques in OpenCCG: Detecting Infeasible Composites in Sentence Generation

Maximilian Schwenger, Álvaro Torralba, Jörg Hoffmann,
David Howcroft, and Vera Demberg

Saarland University,
Saarbrücken, Germany
schwenger@stud.uni-saarland.de, {torralba,hoffmann}@cs.uni-saarland.de,
{howcroft,vera}@coli.uni-saarland.de

Abstract. OpenCCG sentence generation is a prominent approach to *surface realization* – choosing the formulation of a sentence – via search. Such searches often visit many *infeasible* composites (partial sentences), not part of any complete sentence because their grammar category cannot be extended to a sentence in a way covering exactly the desired sentence meaning. Formulating the completion of a composite into a sentence as finding a solution path in a large state-transition system, we exhibit a connection to AI Planning, and we design a compilation from OpenCCG into planning allowing to detect infeasible OpenCCG composites via AI Planning dead-end detection methods. Our experiments show that this can filter out large fractions of infeasible states in, and thus benefit the performance of, complex surface realization processes.

1 Introduction

OpenCCG sentence generation is a prominent approach to surface realization via search [22, 23]. It is based on *combinatory categorial grammars (CCG)*, where words from a lexicon are annotated with syntactic *categories* (e. g. **NP** for "noun phrase"), and simple combination rules dictate how categories can be combined. The target of the realization process is a sentence, category **S**, that conveys the desired meaning, formalized in terms of a set of *semantic items*, where each item must be covered exactly once. The search space (a so-called chart realization algorithm, e. g. [11, 2, 3]) traverses collections of partial sentences (composites, so-called *edges*). One important source of complexity in this context are *infeasible* edges, not part of any complete sentence because their category cannot be extended to a sentence in a way covering exactly the remaining semantic items. Our contribution is a new technique to automatically identify, and prune, infeasible OpenCCG edges, via a connection to AI Planning.

Connections between sentence generation and AI Planning were previously established for so-called tree-adjoining grammars [14, 12, 13], showing how to formulate the entire generation problem as planning. Here we design a new connection for combinatory categorial grammars, and we focus on the objective of identifying infeasible edges, keeping the overall generation process in the hands of OpenCCG. This is better suited for surface realization as a planning compilation would be agnostic of sentence-quality measures, such as n-grams, which are difficult, perhaps impossible, to capture with standard AI Planning quality notions like action costs.

We observe that edge feasibility in OpenCCG – the ability to complete an edge e_0 into a sentence – can be formulated in terms of a state-transition system. We design a compilation of that ability into an AI Planning task Π, where unsolvability of Π – the absence of a path to the planning goal – implies infeasibility of e_0. Applying dead-end detection algorithms from AI Planning (e. g. [6, 9, 8, 19]) to the compiled task Π, and doing so for every edge e_0 during the OpenCCG realization process, then allows to detect and filter out infeasible edges. Our experiments show that this can filter out large fractions of infeasible edges in, and thus benefit the performance of, complex realization processes.

2 Background and State-Transition System Notation

We briefly introduce background and basic notations for OpenCCG and planning, in a manner geared at our compilation techniques.

2.1 OpenCCG

Combinatory categorial grammar (CCG) is a grammar formalism, which, in a nutshell, assigns *(syntactic) categories* to words or sequences thereof, and provides a set of *combination rules* to combine these. Categories can be either atomic, e. g. noun phrase $\mathbf{NP}$, or complex, e. g. $\mathbf{NP/N}$, where a slash indicates that the sequence $\mathbf{NP/N}$ $\mathbf{N}$ can be combined, via application of the *forward application* rule, to obtain a noun phrase. A backslash requires the combination partner, in *backward application*, to be on the left hand side. As an example, consider the sentence `Winter is coming`, where `Winter` as proper name has category $\mathbf{NP}$, `is` as verb modifier has category $\mathbf{S\backslash NP/(S\backslash NP)}$, and `coming` as intransitive verb has category $\mathbf{S\backslash NP}$. We can combine `is coming` to acquire $\mathbf{S\backslash NP}$, and a combination thereof with `Winter` results in a sentence, i. e., in category $\mathbf{S}$. There are also unary rules, allowing to change a word sequence's category on its own, to enable different combinations.

In OpenCCG's realization process, a logical formula consisting of a conjunction of elementary predications – the *semantic items* – is transformed into a sentence covering the semantic items. In this process, a *lexicon* provides entries – words associated with categories – potentially useful in terms of their semantics. Composed entries, enriched with additional information, are called *edges* during the search.[1]

Towards our compilation, we next give notations for OpenCCG, and OpenCCG realization, already following AI Planning terminology. In doing so, we will not keep track of the word sequences in edges, and we will not incorporate any notion of word-sequence quality. This is because the purpose of our work merely is to filter out infeasible edges. We specify only those aspects relevant to that purpose.

We refer to the input of the realization process as an *OpenCCG task*, notated $\Omega = (C_0^\Omega, SI^\Omega, R^\Omega, s_I^\Omega, e_G^\Omega)$. Here, C_0^Ω is the finite set of atomic categories c_0. SI^Ω is the

[1] We find the name clash with "edges" in a graph unfortunate, but stick to this terminology here as it is standard in the OpenCCG literature.

finite set of semantic items si. R^{Ω} is the set of combination rules. We will denote the set of *all* categories, that can be formed from C_0^{Ω} through applying the rules R^{Ω}, by C^{Ω}. s_I^{Ω} is what we call a *state*, a set of *edges*, namely those edges already reached in the state. s_I^{Ω} specifically is the *initial state*. An edge e is a pair (c,σ) where $c \in C^{\Omega}$ is a category and $\sigma \subseteq SI^{\Omega}$ is the subset of semantic items *covered* by e (which we will also refer to as the edge's *coverage*). We denote the set of all edges by E^{Ω}. The initial state $s_I^{\Omega} \subseteq E^{\Omega}$ corresponds to the words in the lexicon. Finally, e_G^{Ω} is the *goal edge*, defined as $e_G^{\Omega} = (\mathbf{S}, SI^{\Omega})$.

Given this input, OpenCCG realization conducts a search – a chart realization process – over the possible constructions of new edges from previous ones. Each step of the search either applies a unary rule to an edge already reached, i. e., an edge contained in the current state; or applies a combination rule to a pair of edges $e_1 = (c_1, \sigma_1)$ and $e_2 = (c_2, \sigma_2)$ from the current state, where c_1 and c_2 can be combined, and the truth value assignments have *empty overlap*, $\sigma_1 \cap \sigma_2 = \emptyset$. The resulting new edge is added into the outcome state. The details of how this search process is organized are not relevant to our purpose. Relevant to us are the states and their transitions, which we notate as Ω's *OpenCCG state space*, $\Theta^{\Omega} = (S^{\Omega}, T^{\Omega}, s_I^{\Omega}, S_G^{\Omega})$. Here, $S^{\Omega} = \mathcal{P}(E^{\Omega})$ is the set of all possible states; $T^{\Omega} \subseteq S^{\Omega} \times S^{\Omega}$ contains the transitions over states, as just explained; s_I^{Ω} is the initial state; and $S_G^{\Omega} := \{s_G^{\Omega} \in S^{\Omega} \mid e_G^{\Omega} \in s_G^{\Omega}\}$, the *goal states*, are those containing e_G^{Ω}. We say that a state s^{Ω} is *reachable* in Θ^{Ω} if there is a transition path from s_I^{Ω} to s^{Ω} in Θ^{Ω}. The reachable states in Θ^{Ω} correspond to the OpenCCG search space. We say that Ω is *solvable* if Θ^{Ω} contains a reachable goal state.

Formulating our example above in this manner, say the semantic items SI^{Ω} are $\{\text{Winter}, \text{be}, \text{comes}\}$. Say the lexicon contains exactly the three words needed, so that the initial state s_I^{Ω} contains the edges $(\mathbf{NP}, \{\text{Winter}\})$, $(\mathbf{S}\backslash\mathbf{NP}/(\mathbf{S}\backslash\mathbf{NP}), \{\text{be}\})$, and $(\mathbf{S}\backslash\mathbf{NP}, \{\text{come}\})$. A solution to Θ^{Ω} then is the path $s_I^{\Omega} \rightarrow s_1^{\Omega} \rightarrow s_2^{\Omega}$ where $s_1^{\Omega} = s_I^{\Omega} \cup \{(\mathbf{S}\backslash\mathbf{NP}, \{\text{be}, \text{come}\})\}$ and $s_2^{\Omega} = s_1^{\Omega} \cup \{(\mathbf{S}, \{\text{Winter}, \text{be}, \text{come}\})\}$.

We say that an edge e_0 is *feasible* in an OpenCCG task Ω iff, in the OpenCCG state space Θ^{Ω}, there is a reachable goal state $s_G^{\Omega} \in S_G^{\Omega}$ *containing a derived tree* T_0 for e_G^{Ω} where e_0 appears in T_0. Here, the derived tree T for an edge e is a tree combining edges to get from elements of s_I^{Ω} to e; and a state s^{Ω} contains T if all edges in T are elements of s^{Ω}. In other words, e_0 is feasible if it forms part of a derived tree for a complete sentence. Otherwise, e_0 is *infeasible*.

2.2 AI Planning

We consider *STRIPS Planning* [5], over Boolean variables (facts), extended with *conditional effects* [17]. This has wide-spread support in modern planning techniques, and matches the needs of our desired OpenCCG compilation.

A *planning task* is a tuple $\Pi = (F^{\Pi}, A^{\Pi}, s_I^{\Pi}, G^{\Pi})$. Here, F^{Π} is a finite set of *facts*; $s_I^{\Pi} \subseteq F^{\Pi}$ is the *initial state* (the facts initially true); and G^{Π} is the *goal* (the facts we need to be true at the end). A^{Π} is a finite set of *actions*. Each action $a \in A^{\Pi}$ is a tuple $(pre_a, add_a, del_a, CEff_a)$ where $pre_a \subseteq F^{\Pi}$ is the action's *precondition*, $add_a \subseteq F^{\Pi}$ is the action's *add list*, $del_a \subseteq F^{\Pi}$ is the action's *delete list*, and $CEff_a$ is the action's finite set of *conditional effects*. Each $e \in CEff_a$ is a triple (con_e, add_e, del_e) of fact sets, namely the effect's *condition*, *add list*, and *delete list* respectively.

Given a planning task Π, the task's *state space* is a tuple $\Theta^\Pi = (S^\Pi, T^\Pi, s_I^\Pi, S_G^\Pi)$. Here, $S^\Pi = \mathcal{P}(F^\Pi)$ is the set of all possible states, i. e., fact subsets interpreted as those facts currently true; s_I^Π is Π's initial state; and $S_G^\Pi := \{s_G \in S^\Pi \mid G^\Pi \subseteq s_G\}$ are the *goal states*, where Π's goal is true. The state transitions $T^\Pi \subseteq S^\Pi \times S^\Pi$ arise from action applications. Action a is *applicable* in state s if $pre_a \subseteq s$; in that case, the outcome state is defined as $s' := (s \cup add_a \cup \bigcup_{e \in CEff_a : con_a \subseteq s} add_e) \setminus (del_a \cup \bigcup_{e \in CEff_a : con_a \subseteq s} del_e)$. In other words, s' results from s by including the add lists of the action plus those effects whose condition holds in s, and afterwards removes the delete lists of the action and those effects.[2] We say that Π is *solvable* if Θ^Π contains a reachable goal state.

3 Partial Compilation of OpenCCG Sentence Generation into AI Planning

There is a correspondence between AI Planning and OpenCCG realization – at the level of category combination rules and semantic item coverage – in that both require to reach a goal, from an initial state, in a transition system described in terms of actions/transition rules. We aim at exploiting this connection, via a *compilation* from OpenCCG into AI Planning, for automatic filtering of infeasible edges.

Our compilation is *partial* in that it does not attempt to preserve OpenCCG edge reachability exactly. The compilation makes approximations – losing information – aimed at practically viability. It consists of (1) a finite approximation of the set of reachable categories; (2) a planning task capturing solvability of Ω, modulo approximation (1) plus an approximation of semantic coverage; (3) a modified planning task capturing edge feasibility. We introduce these constructions in this order.

3.1 Finite Approximations of Reachable Categories

In CCG, combination rules specify how to create new categories from old ones. It is possible in principle to simulate this behavior in terms of AI Planning actions, designed to emulate the behavior of CCG combination rules. But this yields large and complex planning encodings, and it is not clear how to exploit those effectively. Therefore, here we take a different approach, pre-compiling all combined (non-atomic) categories that will be considered by the planning process. Our starting point is what we call the *category space*, capturing all possible categories and compositions:

Definition 1. *Let $\Omega = (C_0^\Omega, SI^\Omega, R^\Omega, s_I^\Omega, e_G^\Omega)$ be an OpenCCG task. The* category space *of Ω is the pair $(C^\Omega, \gamma^\Omega)$ where $\gamma^\Omega : C^\Omega \times C^\Omega \cup C^\Omega \mapsto \mathcal{P}(C^\Omega)$ is the partial function where $c' \in \gamma^\Omega(c)$ iff c can be transformed into c' using a unary rule from R^Ω, and $c' \in \gamma^\Omega(c_1, c_2)$ iff c_1 and c_2 can be combined into c' using a binary rule from R^Ω.*

Note that γ^Ω is a function onto subsets of possible outcome categories, rather than onto a unique outcome category, as several different rules may be applicable to the same

[2] For some purposes, one needs to design a special treatment for conflicting effects, adding vs. deleting the same fact. This will not be relevant in our context.

input categories. Note further that, in the presence of unary rules (like type raising) which are always applicable in CCG, the category space is infinite. To compile it into a finite planning task, we need to restrict ourselves to a finite sub-space. We do so via a size-bound parameter k, in an optimistic vs. a pessimistic manner:

Definition 2. *Let $\Omega = (C_0^\Omega, SI^\Omega, R^\Omega, s_I^\Omega, e_G^\Omega)$ be an OpenCCG task. Let k be a natural number. For $c \in C^\Omega$, let the* degree *of c, denoted $\#(c)$, be the overall number of slashes and backslashes in c. By $C^\Omega[k] := \{c \in C^\Omega \mid \#(c) \leq k\} \cup \{*\}$, we denote the set of all categories whose degree is at most k, plus the* wildcard *symbol $*$.*

The pessimistic category space *of Ω given k is the pair $(C^\Omega[k], \gamma^{-\Omega})$ where $\gamma^{-\Omega}$ is defined like γ^Ω but replacing any category c' where $\#(c') > k$ by $*$. The* optimistic category space *of Ω given k is the pair $(C^\Omega[k], \gamma^{+\Omega})$ where $\gamma^{+\Omega}$ is defined like γ^Ω but replacing any category c' where $\#(c') > k$ by $*$; and including $c' \in \gamma^\Omega(*)$ whenever $\gamma^\Omega(c) = c'$; and including $c' \in \gamma^\Omega(c_1, *)$ whenever $\gamma^\Omega(c_1, c_2) = c'$; and including $c' \in \gamma^\Omega(*, c_2)$ whenever $\gamma^\Omega(c_1, c_2) = c'$.*

In other words, we cut off the generation of categories once their degree exceeds a user-defined threshold k. In the pessimistic (under-approximating) variant, no further combinations are possible behind $*$. In the optimistic (over-approximating) variant, all combinations are possible behind $*$.[3]

Say that, in our example, the lexicon contains only the words $(\mathbf{S}\backslash\mathbf{NP}, \{\text{come}\})$ and $(\mathbf{S}\backslash\mathbf{NP}/(\mathbf{S}\backslash\mathbf{NP}), \{\text{be}\})$. If we set $k := 3$, then $\gamma^{+\Omega}$ preserves γ^Ω sufficiently to determine that $\mathbf{S}$ cannot be reached from the initial state categories. For $k := 2$, however, $\mathbf{S}\backslash\mathbf{NP}/(\mathbf{S}\backslash\mathbf{NP})$ is replaced by $*$, and we can reach $\mathbf{S}$ by "pretending" that $*$ stands for $\mathbf{NP}$.

The optimistic approximation variant preserves solutions and can be used to provide guarantees, i. e., using our edge-feasibility compilation below, to prune only edges that are indeed infeasible. The pessimistic variant does not provide that guarantee, but tends to be more successful in practice as we will show in Section 5. Observe that the approximations approach γ^Ω from opposite sides, in the sense that they are coarsest for $k = 1$, and become more precise as k grows, $\gamma^{+\Omega}$ getting less optimistic and $\gamma^{-\Omega}$ getting less pessimistic. The approximations converge to γ^Ω in that, for any finite sub-space of $(C^\Omega, \gamma^\Omega)$, there is a k so that both approximations are exact. In terms of edge pruning, this means that the optimistic variant prunes more for larger k, and eventually is precise enough to find any edge that can be pruned; while the pessimistic variant prunes less for larger k, and eventually is precise enough to preserve any edge that cannot be pruned (in particular: precise enough to preserve any one solution).

3.2 Planning Compilation for Solvability

To capture solvability relative to the optimistic/pessimistic finite category space approximation, our compiled planning task combines facts keeping track of category creation

[3] One can (and our implementation does) define $\gamma^{+\Omega}$ in a more fine-grained manner, replacing only the *sub*-categories behind the threshold k with $*$, and accordingly being less generous in the over-approximation of γ. As this refined version is cumbersome to spell out formally, and leads to similar results in practice, we omit this here.

with facts keeping track of semantic coverage. Here again we face a design choice: we could, in principle, keep track of the actual category/coverage pairs, i. e., of edges. This would allow us to check for empty overlap when combining two edges. However, that would (a) again yield rather large planning encodings, and (b) require the AI Planning dead-end detection method to be able to reason about delete lists. The most canonical dead-end detection method, that we employ here, does not qualify for (b), so we can just as well circumvent (a). We do so by abstracting from edges, associating a category c with a semantic item si if *at least one* reached edge has category c and covers si. We compile this into a planning task as follows:

Definition 3. *Let* $\Omega = (C_0^\Omega, SI^\Omega, R^\Omega, s_I^\Omega, e_G^\Omega)$ *be an OpenCCG task. Let* k *be a natural number. The* optimistic solvability-compilation *is the planning task* $\Pi^{+\Omega}[k] = (F^\Pi, A^\Pi, s_I^\Pi, G^\Pi)$ *where:*

(i) $F^\Pi = \{c \mid c \in C^\Omega[k]\} \cup \{c[si] \mid c \in C^\Omega[k], si \in SI^\Omega\}$.
(ii) $s_I^\Pi = \{c \mid e = (c,\sigma) \in s_I^\Omega\} \cup \{c[si] \mid e = (c,\sigma) \in s_I^\Omega, si \in \sigma\}$.
(iii) $G^\Pi = \{\mathbf{S}\} \cup \{\mathbf{S}[si] \mid si \in SI^\Omega\}$.
(iv) $A^\Pi = \{a[c,c'] \mid \gamma^{+\Omega}(c) = c'\} \cup \{a[c_1,c_2,c'] \mid \gamma^{+\Omega}(c_1,c_2) = c'\}$, *where:*
   (a) $a[c,c'] := (\{c\},\{c'\},\emptyset,\{(\{c[si]\},\{c'[si]\},\emptyset) \mid si \in SI^\Omega\})$.
   (b) $a[c_1,c_2,c'] := (\{c_1,c_2\},\{c'\},\emptyset,\{(\{c_j[si]\},\{c'[si]\},\emptyset) \mid j \in \{1,2\}, si \in SI^\Omega\})$.

The pessimistic solvability-compilation *is the planning task* $\Pi^{-\Omega}[k]$*, defined like* $\Pi^{+\Omega}[k]$ *but using* $\gamma^{-\Omega}$.

Items (i)–(iii) should be easy to understand: in the compiled planning task, facts c indicate whether category c has been reached yet, and facts $c[si]$ indicate whether c covers si yet; in the initial state, these flags are set according to s_I^Ω, i. e., according to the words in the lexicon; the goal is to have a sentence covering the entire semantics. To understand item (iv), recall that actions have the form $(pre_a, add_a, del_a, CEff_a)$. In item (iv a), encoding unary rule applications $\gamma^{+\Omega}(c) = c'$, the precondition is $\{c\}$ and the (unconditional) add list is $\{c'\}$, effectively saying that, if c is already reached, then applying the action (the rule) yields c'. The conditional effects simply transfer, for each si, the coverage from c (if already reached) to c'. The encoding of binary rules in item (iv b) is similar.

Note that, as indicated above, the delete lists in the compilation are empty. On the one hand, this corresponds to the monotonic nature of the OpenCCG search space, where new edges are being added without removing the old ones. On the other hand, delete effects *would* be needed to capture empty coverage overlap in combination-rule applications. Yet, as explained, in the present approach we forsake that information as our dead-end detector would not be able to handle it anyhow.

Theorem 1. *Let* Ω *be an OpenCCG task. Let* k *be a natural number. If* Ω *is solvable, then so is* $\Pi^{+\Omega}[k]$.

Proof. The proof compares Ω's state space $\Theta^\Omega = (S^\Omega, T^\Omega, s_I^\Omega, S_G^\Omega)$ with that of $\Pi^{+\Omega}[k]$. Denote the latter by $\Theta = (S, T, s_I, S_G)$. Define the mapping $\alpha : S^\Omega \mapsto S$ as $\alpha(s^\Omega) := \{c \mid e = (c,\sigma) \in s^\Omega\} \cup \{c[si] \mid e = (c,\sigma) \in s^\Omega, si \in \sigma\}$. As $\alpha^{+\Omega}$ over-approximates the category combinations in α^Ω, it is easy to see that transitions are preserved by α, i. e., whenever $(s_1^\Omega, s_2^\Omega) \in T^\Omega$, we have $(\alpha(s_1^\Omega), \alpha(s_2^\Omega)) \in T$. Furthermore, goal states are preserved, i. e., whenever $s^\Omega \in S_G^\Omega$, we have $\alpha(s^\Omega) \in S_G$. Finally, $\alpha(s_I^\Omega) = s_I$. The claim follows.

Given Theorem 1, if $\Pi^{+\Omega}[k]$ is *not* solvable, i. e., if an AI Planning dead-end detector is able to detect that this is so, then we can safely conclude that Ω is not solvable either. The pessimistic compilation $\Pi^{-\Omega}[k]$ does not give that guarantee.

For illustration, consider again the example variant where the lexicon contains only the words $(\mathbf{S}\backslash\mathbf{NP}/(\mathbf{S}\backslash\mathbf{NP}), \{\text{be}\})$ and $(\mathbf{S}\backslash\mathbf{NP}, \{\text{come}\})$, so Ω is unsolvable. Then $\Pi^{+\Omega}[3]$ is unsolvable as **S** cannot be reached using $\gamma^{+\Omega}$, cf. above. $\Pi^{+\Omega}[2]$ also is unsolvable, because the semantic item "Winter" cannot be covered; but if we remove that semantic item from the OpenCCG task (and thus from $\Pi^{+\Omega}[2]$), then $\Pi^{+\Omega}[2]$ has a one-step solution combining the two initial-state categories.

3.3 Planning Compilation for Edge Feasibility

The above compilation provides a necessary criterion for an OpenCCG task to be solvable. However, our actual purpose requires a necessary criterion for an OpenCCG *edge* e_0 to be *feasible*, i. e., to form part of a solution. This can be achieved by a simple modification of the compilation, propagating markers to make sure that e_0's category is used in the solution:[4]

Definition 4. *Let* $\Omega = (C_0^\Omega, SI^\Omega, R^\Omega, s_I^\Omega, e_G^\Omega)$ *be an OpenCCG task, and let* $e_0 = (c_0, \sigma_0)$ *be an edge in* Ω. *Let* k *be a natural number. The* optimistic feasibility-compilation *is the planning task* $\Pi^{+\Omega}[k, e_0] = (F^\Pi, A^\Pi, s_I^\Pi, G^\Pi)$ *where:*

(i) $F^\Pi = \{c, c[0] \mid c \in C^\Omega[k]\} \cup \{c[si] \mid c \in C^\Omega[k], si \in SI^\Omega\}$.
(ii) $s_I^\Pi = \{c_0[0]\} \cup \{c \mid e = (c,\sigma) \in s_I^\Omega, \sigma \cap \sigma_0 = \emptyset\} \cup \{c[si] \mid e = (c,\sigma) \in s_I^\Omega, \sigma \cap \sigma_0 = \emptyset, si \in \sigma\}$.
(iii) $G^\Pi = \{\mathbf{S}, \mathbf{S}[0]\} \cup \{\mathbf{S}[si] \mid si \in SI^\Omega\}$.
(iv) $A^\Pi = \{a[c, c'] \mid \gamma^{+\Omega}(c) = c'\} \cup \{a[c_1, c_2, c'] \mid \gamma^{+\Omega}(c_1, c_2) = c'\}$, *where:*
  (a) $a[c, c'] := (\{c\}, \{c'\}, \emptyset, \{(\{c[0]\}, \{c'[0]\}, \emptyset)\} \cup \{(\{c[si]\}, \{c'[si]\}, \emptyset) \mid si \in SI^\Omega\})$.
  (b) $a[c_1, c_2, c'] := (\{c_1, c_2\}, \{c'\}, \emptyset, \{(\{c_1[0]\}, \{c'[0]\}, \emptyset), (\{c_2[0]\}, \{c'[0]\}, \emptyset)\} \cup \{(\{c_j[si]\}, \{c'[si]\}, \emptyset) \mid j \in \{1, 2\}, si \in SI^\Omega\})$.

The pessimistic feasibility-compilation *is* $\Pi^{-\Omega}[k, e_0]$, *defined like* $\Pi^{+\Omega}[k, e_0]$ *but using* $\gamma^{-\Omega}$.

Relative to Definition 3, we add the $c[0]$ markers to keep track of whether an ancestor of c uses e_0's category. The initial state includes this marker only for e_0's own category c_0, the goal is for **S** to be marked. The actions propagate the markers through conditional effects, marking the outcome category c' if at least one of the input categories is already marked. The additions "$\sigma \cap \sigma_0 = \emptyset$" in (ii) introduce a limited form of empty coverage overlap reasoning, excluding in the initial state those edges whose semantics overlaps with e_0 (and that thus won't be used in a solution incorporating e_0).

[4] In this definition, the modifications relative to Definition 3 are shown in red for the benefit of on-screen reading.

Theorem 2. *Let Ω be an OpenCCG task, and let e_0 be an edge in Ω. Let k be a natural number. If e_0 is feasible in Ω, then $\Pi^{+\Omega}[k, e_0]$ is solvable.*

Proof. Say that e_0 is feasible in Ω. Then there is a solution θ to Ω using e_0, and not using any $e \in s_I^\Omega$ whose semantics overlaps with that of e_0. By Theorem 1, $\Pi^{+\Omega}[k]$ is solvable, via a transition path π corresponding to θ. By construction, π is a solution for $\Pi^{+\Omega}[k, e_0]$.

Given Theorem 2, if an AI Planning dead-end detector proves $\Pi^{+\Omega}[k, e_0]$ to be unsolvable, then we can conclude that e_0 is infeasible. The pessimistic compilation $\Pi^{-\Omega}[k, e_0]$ does not give that guarantee.

Say that, in our example, the lexicon contains the words $e_1 = (\mathbf{NP}, \{\text{Winter}\})$, $e_2 = (\mathbf{S\backslash NP/(S\backslash NP)}, \{\text{be}\})$, and $e_3 = (\mathbf{S\backslash NP}, \{\text{come}\})$ as before, but contains also the transitive form of "coming", $e_4 = (\mathbf{(S\backslash NP)/NP}, \{\text{come}\})$, infeasible for our purposes. Consider the edge $e_0 = (\mathbf{S\backslash NP}, \{\text{Winter}, \text{come}\})$, where we combined e_1 with e_4. Consider the compilation $\Pi^{+\Omega}[3, e_0]$: In the initial state, as e_1 overlaps e_0, e_1 is not included. But without **NP**, **S** is unreachable given $\gamma^{+\Omega}$ for $k = 3$, so $\Pi^{+\Omega}[3, e_0]$ is unsolvable and we correctly detect that e_0 is infeasible.[5]

4 Practical Compilation Use and Optimizations

Our idea is to create, and check the solvability of, the compiled planning task $\Pi^{+\Omega}[k, e_0]$ respectively $\Pi^{-\Omega}[k, e_0]$, every time a new edge e_0 is created during the OpenCCG realization process. If the compiled planning task is unsolvable, e_0 is deemed infeasible, and is discarded. This filtering method is provably sound when using $\Pi^{+\Omega}[k, e_0]$. When using $\Pi^{-\Omega}[k, e_0]$, it is a practical heuristic, and converges to sound pruning – eventually preserving the best solution – as k grows.

To realize this approach, we require a method for checking solvability of planning tasks. In general, however, deciding solvability ("plan existence") is **PSPACE**-complete [1]. For fast solvability detection, planning research therefore concentrates on polynomial-time solvable fragments of the plan existence problem. The most widespread such fragment is the one where all delete lists are required to be empty (e. g. [1, 6, 9]). Hence the design of our compilation, which incorporates approximations resulting in empty delete lists. For planning tasks with empty delete lists, plan existence can be decided in time low-order polynomial in the size of the task, using so-called *relaxed planning graphs* [9].

Though polynomial time, testing delete-free plan existence does incur a runtime overhead, especially in our context where we need to do so for every edge during realization. Efficient implementation is therefore important. One key to this is the re-use of information/computation shared across individual tests. First, every call to sentence realization based on the same lexicon shares the same category space. Hence we can

[5] Note that the same is not true for $k = 2$; and neither for e_4 because, there, ignoring overlap in rule applications means that e_1 could be used twice. These are weaknesses of our current approach, which could potentially be tackled by more informed compilations. We get back to this in the conclusion.

build the category space approximation, $(C^{\Omega}[k], \gamma^{+\Omega})$ respectively $(C^{\Omega}[k], \gamma^{-\Omega})$, *offline*, just once for the lexicon at hand, prior to realization. Second, the feasibility compilations for individual edges e_0 during the same realization process are identical except for their initial states. So, during a realization process, we create a compiled task just once and adapt it minimally for each test.

Finally, (a) the action set in $\Pi^{+\Omega}[k, e_0]$ respectively $\Pi^{-\Omega}[k, e_0]$ is fully determined by $\gamma^{+\Omega}$ respectively $\gamma^{-\Omega}$ along with the set of semantic items SI^{Ω}; while (b) for the maintenance of semantic coverage and $c[0]$ markers, instead of the compilation via conditional effects as specified, one can implement a simple special-case handling in the standard relaxed planning graph solvability test. Taking these two observations together, we can generate the action set completely offline. Online, prior to a realization process, we merely need to read in the actions and setup the marker-maintenance data structures.

5 Experiments

As our main test base for experimentation, we used the SPaRKy Restaurant Corpus (we also ran preliminary experiments with some other test bases, which we get back to below). SPaRKy is one of the only published resources for NLG which provides intermediate representations in addition to system inputs and outputs, and quality ratings for those outputs. Originally introduced by Walker et al. [21], Nakatsu and White [16] developed a CCG grammar for this dataset which spans both the sentence and the discourse levels. The domain of the corpus is restaurant descriptions, including prices, kind of food, decor, service, etc. In this work we use the a set of 431 test instances developed for the contrast-enhanced version of the grammar presented in Howcroft, Nakatsu, & White [10]. The lexicon in this testbed includes 193 words and the grammar is capable of producing a wide variety of texts of varying lengths. Of the 431 OpenCCG realization tasks, 61 *recommendation tasks* require generating a text recommending a single restaurant, while 370 *comparison tasks* require generating a text comparing two or more restaurants with each other. As these instances correspond to the generation of entire text paragraphs, they are complex enough to be interesting use cases for our techniques. This pertains in particular to the comparison tasks, where the required text is longer.

In preliminary tests with the optimistic approximation variant, the pruning was too weak to pay off, i. e., too few edges were pruned to get a benefit. We therefore concentrate here on pruning with the pessimistic approximation variant, where small values of k may prune too aggressively, while large values of k yield more reliable pruning yet incur a larger runtime overhead. All experiments were run on a cluster of machines with Intel Xeon E5-2660 processors running at 2.2 GHz. The runtime/memory limit was set to 30 minutes/4 GB for each sentence generation task, i. e., for each benchmark instance.

As a simple measure of performance, we focus on the runtime spent by the OpenCCG chart realization process until the first solution – the first edge of category **S** covering all semantic items – is generated. Figure 1 shows coverage, i. e., the number of benchmark instances where a solution was found, as a function of runtime. We distinguish between

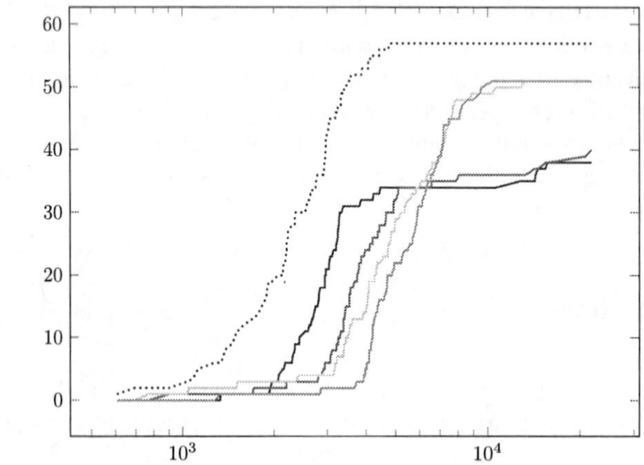

(a)

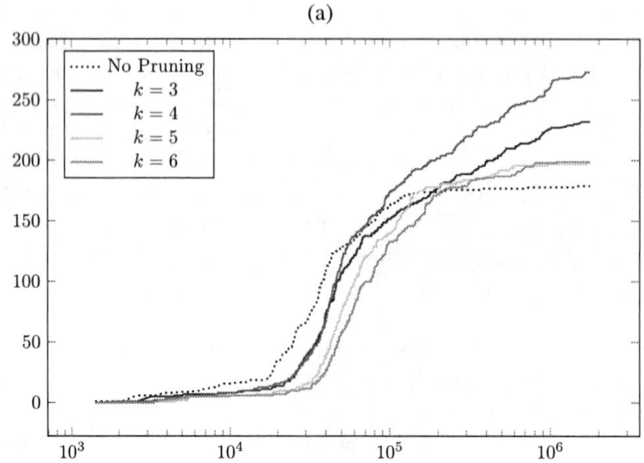

(b)

Fig. 1. Coverage, i. e., the number of sentence generation tasks to which a solution was found, as a function of runtime on SPaRKy (a) recommendation tasks and (b) comparison tasks. A data point (x, y) means that y tasks are solved within a time limit of x milliseconds. "No pruning" is the baseline OpenCCG search without pruning; "$k = n$" considers our pessimistic pruning with parameter k, i. e., the $\Pi^{-\Omega}[k, e_0]$ compilation, on every edge e_0 during search, pruning e_0 if $\Pi^{-\Omega}[k, e_0]$ is unsolvable.

(a) recommendation vs. (b) comparison tasks as these are different in nature and yield very different performance profiles.

Regarding (a), we see that these tasks are essentially too easy for our pruning method to pay off: the runtime overhead of repeatedly checking the solvability of $\Pi^{-\Omega}[k, e_0]$ outweighs the gain from pruning, so that fewer tasks are solved within the same runtime limits. The restaurant comparison tasks (b), however, are more challenging (notice the different x-axis scales in (a) and (b)), and the picture is different: in the much larger search spaces, the pruning impact is stronger. For runtime limits > 56 seconds, the coverage of $k = 4$ pruning exceeds that without pruning. For runtime limits > 206 seconds, all settings of k exceed the baseline. Note here that the value of k controls the trade-off between accuracy (better with large k) and runtime overhead (better with small k). In SPaRKy restaurant comparison tasks, $k = 4$ is the sweet spot of that trade off. At our maximum time limit of $x = 30$ minutes, $k = 4$ pruning increases coverage from 179 instances without pruning, to 273 with pruning, an increase of 52%.

As the pessimistic compilation does not guarantee that pruned edges are actually infeasible, the pruning may adversely affect the quality of the sentences generated. As k gets larger, this danger decreases as the pruning becomes more accurate. In SPaRKy, it turns out that $k = 4$ is not only best in terms of runtime performance, but is also enough to avoid any deterioration in sentence quality. Of the 215 instances solved by both the baseline and $k = 4$ (across recommendation and comparison tasks), in 137 cases the two realizations are identical. In the remainining 78 cases, the realizations differ only in using the word "just" vs. the word "only", so that the version with pruning does exactly as well as the baseline.

Going beyond solutions, there also are cases where OpenCCG produces a *partial solution*, an edge of category S that covers only a subset of the semantic items. This can still be useful if, e. g., four instead of five restaurants are being compared. Our $k = 4$ pruning has clear advantages in terms of the ability to find such partial solutions. Of the 97 cases where neither $k = 4$ nor the baseline find a complete solution, $k = 4$ provides a partial solution in 81 cases, the baseline in 52 cases. In all 21 cases where only the baseline finds a complete solution, $k = 4$ finds a partial solution. In contrast, of the 98 cases where only $k = 4$ finds a complete solution, in 59 cases the baseline does not manage to find a partial solution.

We also ran experiments on some other test bases [20, 18, 15], yet as the text paragraphs to be generated were comparatively small, similarly to SPaRKy recommendation tasks our pruning methods generally did not pay off. Conversely, in the CCGBank [7], our category space approximations consumed excessive amounts of memory. For practical viability in such large bases, either additional implementation tricks, or more intelligent abstractions (not just enumerating all categories up to a fixed degree), would be required.

6 Conclusion

Sentence generation as search relates deeply to AI Planning in that, at least as far as grammatical and semantical correctness is concerned, it is essentially a reachability problem in a large discrete transition system. This connection has been made before, and we herein propose a new variant and application, detecting infeasible edges in OpenCCG. Our empirical results show promise, though much remains to be done.

In our view, the most pressing and interesting question is *how much information we can efficiently capture and exploit* in this kind of compilation. Our present approach is (a) inflexible in precomputing a category space approximation, and (b) conservative in targeting delete-free planning which is easy to handle. Both design choices sacrifice information, and both may be lifted through more intelligent compilations/abstractions, paired with more advanced dead-end detection on the AI Planning side, as exhibited e. g. in the inaugural unsolvability-detection planning competition `http://unsolve-ipc.eng.unimelb.edu.au/`.

From a broader point of view, we believe that AI Planning, and AI search techniques more generally, can be a crucial piece in the puzzle for achieving practical sentence generation with complex optimization objectives [4].

References

1. Tom Bylander. The computational complexity of propositional STRIPS planning. *Artificial Intelligence*, 69(1–2):165–204, 1994.
2. Aoife Cahill and Josef van Genabith. Robust pcfg-based generation using automatically acquired LFG approximations. In Nicoletta Calzolari, Claire Cardie, and Pierre Isabelle, editors, *Proceedings of the 21st International Conference on Computational Linguistics (ACL'06)*. ACL, 2006.
3. John A. Carroll and Stephan Oepen. High efficiency realization for a wide-coverage unification grammar. In *Natural Language Processing–IJCNLP*, pages 165–176, 2005.
4. Vera Demberg, Jörg Hoffmann, David Howcroft, Dietrich Klakow, and Alvaro Torralba. Search challenges in natural language generation with complex optimization objectives. *KI – Künstliche Intelligenz*, 30:63–69, 2016.
5. Richard E. Fikes and Nils Nilsson. STRIPS: A new approach to the application of theorem proving to problem solving. *Artificial Intelligence*, 2:189–208, 1971.
6. Patrik Haslum and Hector Geffner. Admissible heuristics for optimal planning. In S. Chien, R. Kambhampati, and C. Knoblock, editors, *Proceedings of the 5th International Conference on Artificial Intelligence Planning Systems (AIPS'00)*, pages 140–149, Breckenridge, CO, 2000. AAAI Press, Menlo Park.
7. Julia Hockenmaier and Mark Steedman. Ccgbank: A corpus of ccg derivations and dependency structures extracted from the penn treebank. *Computational Linguistics*, 33(3):355–396, September 2007.
8. Jörg Hoffmann, Peter Kissmann, and Álvaro Torralba. "Distance"? Who Cares? Tailoring merge-and-shrink heuristics to detect unsolvability. In Thorsten Schaub, editor, *Proceedings of the 21st European Conference on Artificial Intelligence (ECAI'14)*, Prague, Czech Republic, August 2014. IOS Press.
9. Jörg Hoffmann and Bernhard Nebel. The FF planning system: Fast plan generation through heuristic search. *Journal of Artificial Intelligence Research*, 14:253–302, 2001.
10. David Howcroft, Crystal Nakatsu, and Michael White. Enhancing the expression of contrast in the sparky restaurant corpus. In *Proceedings of the 14th European Workshop on Natural Language Generation (ENLG'13)*, pages 30–39, 2013.
11. Martin Kay. Chart generation. In Aravind K. Joshi and Martha Palmer, editors, *Proceedings of the 34th Annual Meeting of the Association for Computational Linguistics*, pages 200–204. Morgan Kaufmann / ACL, 1996.

12. Alexander Koller and Jörg Hoffmann. Waking up a sleeping rabbit: On natural-language sentence generation with ff. In Ronen I. Brafman, Hector Geffner, Jörg Hoffmann, and Henry A. Kautz, editors, *Proceedings of the 20th International Conference on Automated Planning and Scheduling (ICAPS'10)*. AAAI Press, 2010.
13. Alexander Koller and Ronald Petrick. Experiences with planning for natural language generation. *Computational Intelligence*, 27(1):23–40, 2011.
14. Alexander Koller and Matthew Stone. Sentence generation as planning. In *Proc. of the 45th Annual Meeting of the Association for Computational Linguistics (ACL'07)*, 2007.
15. Geert-Jan M Kruijff, Pierre Lison, Trevor Benjamin, Henrik Jacobsson, Hendrik Zender, Ivana Kruijff-Korbayová, and Nick Hawes. Situated dialogue processing for human-robot interaction. In *Cognitive Systems*, pages 311–364. Springer, 2010.
16. Crystal Nakatsu and Michael White. Generating with discourse combinatory categorial grammar. *Linguistic Issues in Language Technology*, 4(1), 2010.
17. Edwin P.D. Pednault. ADL: Exploring the middle ground between STRIPS and the situation calculus. In R. Brachman, H. J. Levesque, and R. Reiter, editors, *Principles of Knowledge Representation and Reasoning: Proceedings of the 1st International Conference (KR-89)*, pages 324–331, Toronto, ON, May 1989. Morgan Kaufmann.
18. Stefania Racioppa. Italian ccg grammar for aliz-e. Technical report, DFKI, 2011.
19. Marcel Steinmetz and Jörg Hoffmann. Towards clause-learning state space search: Learning to recognize dead-ends. In Dale Schuurmans and Michael Wellman, editors, *Proceedings of the 30th AAAI Conference on Artificial Intelligence (AAAI'16)*. AAAI Press, February 2016.
20. Jean Vancoppenolle, Eric Tabbert, Gerlof Bouma, and Manfred Stede. A german grammar for generation in openccg. Number 96, pages 145–150, 2011.
21. Marilyn A. Walker, Amanda Stent, François Mairesse, and Rashmi Prasad. Individual and domain adaptation in sentence planning for dialogue. *Journal of Artificial Intelligence Research*, 30:413–456, 2007.
22. Michael White. Efficient realization of coordinate structures in combinatory categorial grammar. *Research on Language and Computation*, 4(1):39–75, 2006.
23. Michael White and Rajakrishnan Rajkumar. Minimal dependency length in realization ranking. In *Proceedings of the 2012 Joint Conference on Empirical Methods in Natural Language Processing and Computational Natural Language Learning*, pages 244–255, 2012.

Automated Data Management Workflow Generation with Ontologies and Planning

PuK 2016 submission

University of Freiburg, Germany
{bwright,mattmuel}@informatik.uni-freiburg.de

Abstract. When working with data management systems, it is often required to specify and model the data within the system. Ontologies are a widely used method of defining data and its relations within a system by defining concepts, properties, and roles. In addition to the definition of the data structures, workflows are required for adding new knowledge to the ontologies. We will show how AI planning can be used to derive such workflows from the ontology, enforcing the closed world assumption required for data management systems.

Keywords: planning, data management, workflow management, ontologies

1 Introduction

Data management deals with all issues arising during the life cycle of data as a resource. One major issue is the definition of the actual data: Which data types are there and what kind of information is to be stored about them. During the development of a data management system for archiving research data, we were confronted with two of these aspects: How should the data be modelled, and how should the workflows for archiving this data be managed. As a solution to the first issue, ontologies where chosen. Ontologies can be used to model the structure of data, the relationships between pieces of data, and its context within an organization (e. g., who created the data). An ontology consists of two parts, the *TBox* which holds the concept, role, and property definitions, and the *ABox* which holds the actual instances of the concepts, roles, and properties. In the *TBox*, concepts and properties are used to model data types. For instance, the concept *Book* can be defined and the property *title* can be added to this concept. Then roles can be added to put the concepts into relations with each other, e. g., a role *isAuthorOf* which puts a person and a book into an authorship relation. In addition to the definition of the data types, *workflows* are needed to add the data to a data management system, and to perform administrative tasks on them. A workflow in the context of ontology-driven data management can be defined as sequence of *assertRole*, *create*, *select* statements which transform the initial *ABox* A into a target *ABox* A' such that $A' \equiv A \cup B$ with B a set of target assertions. Although ontologies operate in an open world context, we require each object that is used for an assertion to be created prior to its first use. This enforces a closed world paradigm required for data management. This requirement introduces acyclic dependencies between the assertions in the workflow, generating a natural ordering of actions to be taken. Additionally, some actions will be taken by humans, introducing some nondeterministic effects to the workflow, which necessitates branching depending on the user input. This has the effect that the sequence in which assertions have to occur is non-trivial. Hoffmann et al. [12] showed that deriving workflows can be achieved by means of AI planning. However, they used SAP's proprietary SAM (Status and Action Management) model for generating the planning domain. We will show how knowledge from an ontology can be translated into a planning task with the goal of finding a sequence of actions which creates the aforementioned assertions. Additionally to the non-trivial sequence of actions, data management systems can consist of hundreds of data types, making the task of modelling each workflow manually very labour intensive. Therefore, an automated approach was chosen for our archival system mentioned above.

Technically speaking, we define a *state* of a workflow as a tuple $s = \langle T, A, C \rangle$, where T is a *TBox*, A is an *ABox*, and C is a set of individuals that were already *created.* We use C to allow working in a closed-world setting where objects need to be created before any assertion about them can be made. Then, a *problem instance* P is an initial state $s_0 = \langle T, A_0, C_0 \rangle$ of a workflow plus a *target assertion* a_0, which is a triple $(i, j) : r$ consisting of two individual names i and j and a role name r. For simplicity, we assume that the initial *TBox* T is fixed and cannot be modified, and that the initial *ABox* A_0 is empty. C_0 may or may not contain any elements. We allow the following modifications of a state $s = \langle T, A, C \rangle$ as part of the workflow we want to construct: A *create* statement creates a new individual not yet in C and adds it to C, and an *assertRole* statement adds a new role assertion to A putting two individuals previously created into a role relationship (for a specific role name r). *Create* statements are only allowed if the individual to be created is not yet in C, and *assertRole* statements are only allowed if the relevant individuals have been created before. A *solution* to P is then a sequence $a_0, \ldots, a_{n-1}$ of *assertRole* and *create* statements producing states $s_1, \ldots, s_n$ such that (i) statement a_i is allowed in state s_i, that (ii) state s_{i+1} results from applying statement a_i to state s_i, $i = 0, \ldots, n-1$, and that (iii) in state $s_n = \langle T, A_n, C_n \rangle$, the target assertion holds, i. e., that $A_n \models a_0$.

Notice that this only allows *linear* workflows where all relevant individuals are either already created (and known to be created) prior to the workflow execution, or explicitly created during the workflow. A more expressive framework would additionally allow *select* statements as part of a workflow, modelling that a user attempts to select a desired individual from a list of known individuals. However, this user interaction would introduce nondeterminism and hence possibly *branching* workflows that we do not yet support, but rather consider to be future work.

In order to obtain a solution to P, we translate P to a planning task $\Pi(P)$ that is solvable if and only if P has a solution and such that every plan $\pi(\Pi(P))$

for $\Pi(P)$ translates back to a solution $\tau(\pi(\Pi(P)))$ to P using an appropriate plan-to-statement-sequence translation function τ.

Motivating Scenario. Ontologies can be used to model a wide range of knowledge. This leads to the issue that for each new ontology, applications working with this knowledge need to be adapted. These applications usually provide some means of adding or manipulating the knowledge in the ontology, implementing workflows defined by individuals or organisations. Manually creating these workflows for large knowledge bases can be very tedious. Therefore, means of generating these workflows automatically provides a major improvement to such systems. Our main motivation arose during the development of a software system for long-term preservation of research data. During this, the requirement for modelling document types together with workflows for their creation arose. Consider for instance an ontology modelling the document type *Article*, with roles putting the article into context, such as a role *isAuthorOf* relating persons to articles, or a role *isFundingAgencyOf* relating funding agencies to articles. One workflow could now describe the action required for adding a new article to the knowledge base. This could consist of uploading a file and selecting a set of authors from a list of people already in the system. Similarly, a list of funding agencies can be selected. Additionally, new people or agencies might need to be added to the knowledge base. What we want to achieve is an automated way of deriving such workflows from the knowledge stored in a given ontology. We would like to emphasize at this point, that this paper presents our preliminary results, and should serve as starting point for discussions and feedback.

2 Related Work

As mentioned in the introduction, Hoffmann et al. [12] showed that AI planning can be used to create workflows for business process management. However, they used SAP's internal SAM model for modelling the business objects, where each business object is associated with status variables and possible actions. In contrast, we do not a-priori associate elements from our ontology to possible actions in our planning domain, but rather generate the actions during the translation process from ontology to PDDL. Bouillet et al. [4] presented a framework which allows the problem to be modelled using OWL ontologies. However, each action is modelled explicitly as an ontology pattern. Even though this provides a very flexible way of defining problem domains, we focus on generating sequences of assertions without their explicit modelling. To our knowledge, no previous work exists focusing on deriving plans for adding new knowledge to an existing ontology, based solely on the existing ontology. A different approach to adding new knowledge to an existing ontology is show in Calvanese et al. [5], who show how actions defined in Knowledge and Action Bases, more precisely state bounded KABs, are used in ADL planning for manipulating the original ontology. However they use a defined set of actions which are on the one hand more flexible, but also introduce additional complexity during the knowledge base modelling. Related work also contains work on automated web service composition via planning [3], discussing which in detail would go beyond the scope of this paper.

3 Background

In this section, we introduce the required background to our work, starting with the definitions used in ontologies followed by an introduction to planning.

3.1 Ontologies

Ontologies can be used to structure knowledge by defining concepts and relationships between concepts, adding structure to otherwise unstructured data. An ontology thereby consists of two parts: The *TBox* holding the definitions outlining the terminology of the knowledge base, and the *ABox* consisting of the elements representing the actual state of knowledge. The terms in the *TBox* are *concepts* which identify individuals as instances of given concepts, and *roles* denoting binary relationships between concepts. In the *ABox*, the *concepts* and *roles* are instantiated in the form of individuals (*concept assertions*) and roles (*role assertions*) [1]. During ontology development, the terms *object property* and *data property* will occur. *Object properties* refer to roles regarding two individuals of the type *concept assertions*, whereas *data properties* refer to relationships between *concept assertions* and *value assertion* (String, Integer, Date, ...). In the remainder of this paper, the term property is only used in the context of the latter. And individuals can be of the form *concept assertion* or a *value assertion*.

Description Language. The description language used in this paper will be $\mathcal{FL}_f^-$, which supports the following concepts: A (atomic concepts), $\top, \bot$ (top and bottom concept), $C \sqcap D$ (intersection), $\forall R.C$ (value restriction), $\exists R.\top$ (limited existential restriction). Additionally, functional roles are supported. Expanding to a more expressive description logic will be part of future work.

3.2 Planning

We translate the search for a successful sequence of assertions to the search for a plan in a corresponding planning task. To model planning tasks, we use the following framework: A planning task consists of a finite set of finite-domain state variables, a finite set of operators with preconditions and effects, an initial state description and a goal condition. To simplify the translation, we translate to a rather expressive fragment of ADL [18] and refer the reader to the literature on how to compile this fragment further down to STRIPS [8] or SAS$^+$ [2]. We allow the following ADL features: negation, disjunction, universal and existential quantification in preconditions, universal and conditional effects, equality, and typing. Our notation in the examples below should be largely self-explanatory. Conditional effects are written as $c \rhd e$ where c is the effect condition and e is the effect.

The semantics of planning tasks is as usual, i. e., a plan is a sequence of applicable operators transforming the initial state to a state satisfying the goal condition. Details can be found in the literature [9, 16]. Notice that we explicitly do not make an open-world assumption on the planning side, but rather assume a closed world as usual in classical planning. This guarantess that planners such as Fast Downward [10] support the language we use. In the following, we will freely switch between schematic and grounded representations, and, for notational convenience, use schematic representations to specify operators resulting from our compilation.

3.3 Open World or Closed World

The closed-world assumption states that everything which is true is also known to be true. In contrast, the open-world assumption states that if something is not known to be true, it may or may not be true. No precise statement can be made. When dealing with ontologies, the open-world assumption is made, which means that knowledge that is not stated in the *ABox* may simply be missing. However, when we deal with AI planning, only knowledge that is known to be true can be treated as being true, i. e., planning makes a closed-world assumption. This has to be taken in to account when translating from ontologies to planning. How this is achieved will be discussed in Section 5.1.

4 Modelling Ontologies for Data Management

To define the data types, first a concept representing this data type needs to be specified. Then all properties and relations need to be defined. This can be achieved using $\mathcal{FL}_f^-$ which allows the definition of properties, roles, and concepts. Some of the properties can be defined as being functional, restricting the amount of these properties each individual of a concept can be associated with to one. Roles are defined in the form of triples consisting of the *domain*, *role*, and *range*, which can be interpreted as concept *domain* is in relation *role* with concept *range*. Instances of concepts and properties shall be called *individuals* from here after. Even though $\mathcal{FL}_f^-$ seems to be a very limited DL, it is expressive enough to define the data types required in our data management system. Additionally to the constructors mentioned in Section 3.1, we can use $\sqsubseteq$ and $\equiv$(concept inclusion and concept equivalence) to create our data type definitions. This allows concepts to be created, properties assigned to these concepts, and concepts to be put into relation with each other. Consider an example: Defining the concepts *Person* and *Book*, properties *name* and *title*, and the role *isAuthor*, we can define a simple ontology describing the data type *Book* as shown in Fig. 1. Yellow boxes represent concepts, and green boxes represent property value types that are needed to define data properties. Solid connections represent role relations (individuals of type *Person* can be in authorship relations to individuals of type *Book*), and similarly, dashed connections represent data properties of the connected concepts (individuals of type *Person* have a name, which is a character string, and similarly, individuals of type *Book* have a title). The numbers 1 and n used as edge labels denote whether the pertinent roles/properties are required to be functional (1) or not (n). Intuitively, there are many ways of defining the same semantic concept or relation. Therefore it is advised to use a generally accepted standard for modelling an ontology. One such standard applicable to data management is the Dublin Core standard [7] which can serve as a starting point, refining it where necessary. Lenzerini [13] gives a nice introduction to the use of ontologies in data-management systems, together with some of the arising issues.

5 From Ontology to Planning Task

We want to faithfully translate the knowledge encoded in a given ontology to a planning task. In this section, the very simple ontology shown in Fig. 1 is used to illustrate the translation from ontology to planning task.

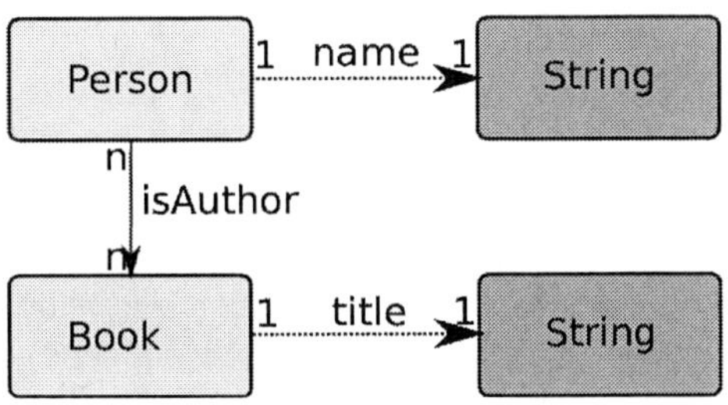

Fig. 1. Sample Ontology

As we are only interested in generalized workflows, we consider the ABox to be empty in the initial state. This will guarantee that we create workflows independently of the current knowledge in the ABox. Using assertions from the ABox would result in workflows specially targeting certain instances from the ABox, making the resulting workflow instance specific. Additionally, editing or deleting assertions from the ontology is currently not supported, and is subject to further research.

5.1 Creating the Planning Domain

Starting from the target assertion, all relevant concepts, properties and roles are identified. In this context, relevant means that the concept, role, or property is in a role or property relation to the target assertion or an element previously identified as relevant. Relevancy is calculated recursively until reaching the top element by traversing all super-class relations encountered.

Concepts and Individuals. For each identified concept C, a type t_C is added to the planning task, and an action a_C for the creation of individuals of this type is added to the set of operators, which marks an individual c of type t_C as created by setting a corresponding predicate *created*(c) to true. This action is needed to bridge the gap between open-world semantics (ontologies) and closed-world semantics (planning). Additionally, the type t_C is populated with a predefined number of objects by mentioning them in the initial state. Those objects may or may not already be *created*, depending on the current state of the ontology. As long as they are not *created*, nothing can be asserted about them. Additionally, for each role and property, a constant of type *role* is added to the set of domain constant symbols. It is noteworthy at this point that we use planning types to both encode different concepts as well as the "meta types" role, concept, property and individual. We do this by creating a typing system defining assertion, role, concept, and individual as elements of type object, and create derived types for each element from the ontology.

When dealing with complex concepts such as $C \sqsubseteq A \sqcap B$ we create types for C, A, and B. Creating an individual of type A and of type B will result in the creation of two separate elements a and b. For the desired result here, it is required to create an individual of type C

Roles. In the ontology, roles are used to describe the relation in which two individuals stand. Similarly, data properties relate individuals to value types. For a uniform treatment, in the planning task, we deal with roles and data properties in the same way and hence focus on describing roles here. The only difference is that data properties are asserted during their concept's creation actions, and roles can be asserted individually. So, in the planning task, we introduce a type *role*, and for each role name r from the ontology, a constant object m_r of type *role*.

Assertions. Assertions define which information is explicitly present in the ontology. TBox assertions state what concepts and roles are defined, and ABox assertions define the concrete individuals and relations of the given concepts and roles stored in the ontology. For the planner to be able to deal with the notion of assertions, we introduce a new type *assertion*. For roles we then define a subtype *roleAssertion* which represents the ontology triples $(i, j) : r$ of individuals i and j and the role r, which can be interpreted as the individual i is r-related to j. For each possible role assertion from the subset of relevant roles we create an object a of type *roleAssertion* and relate the individuals i and j as well as the role r to it. This is achieved by adding the following statements to the initial state of the planning problem: *domain*(a, i), *range*(a, j), and *role*(a, r), which corresponds to the domain, range and role defined in the ontology. Notice that we do not need a type *conceptAssertion*, since we do not allow new concept assertions to be made during the planning process. Rather, each individual is fixed to belong to a certain set of concepts in the initial state of the planning task and this can never change. This process introduces many *roleAssertions* which might never be used, however, since we limit the possible assertions to the ones identified as relevant in the previous step, the amount of assertions to be taken in to account during planning is bounded by the number of relevant assertions, not to the size of the whole ontology. This greatly reduces the overall complexity of the planning task.

Actions. Actions will differ for each ontology, as they are dependent on the concepts, properties and roles. However one action will be consistent over all ontologies and is required for the above mentioned role assertions. An action *assertRole* is therefore defined. It takes as parameters two individuals i and j, and one role name r. It then selects an existing *roleAssertion* which matches these parameters, and marks it as *asserted*, indicating that, as a result of this action, the role is asserted to the ontology's *ABox*.

$$\begin{aligned}
\texttt{Operator} &= \mathit{assertRole}(i : \mathit{individual}, r : \mathit{role}, j : \mathit{individual}) \\
\texttt{pre} &= \mathit{created}(i) \wedge \mathit{created}(j) \\
\texttt{eff} &= \forall a : \mathit{roleAssertion} \\
&\quad \big((\mathit{domain}(a, i) \wedge \mathit{role}(a, r) \wedge \mathit{range}(a, j)) \\
&\quad\quad \rhd \mathit{asserted}(a)\big)
\end{aligned}$$

For each subtype of individual, a create action is required. The create actions for properties are fairly straightforward as the action takes an individual of the creation type as a parameter and marks it as *created* in its effect. This ensures that all properties used in later create or assert actions are created prior to their use, enforcing the required closed-world paradigm.

$$\begin{aligned}
\texttt{Operator} &= \mathit{createProperty}(p : \mathit{property}) \\
\texttt{pre} &= \neg \mathit{created}(p) \\
\texttt{eff} &= \mathit{created}(p)
\end{aligned}$$

Each concept from the ontology requires its own create action, which also takes all its functional properties as parameters. This ensures that the correct properties are assigned to the new instance of the concept. The precondition of the action checks if the passed properties are created prior to their use and are not in use by a different *roleAssertion*, thus not assigned to another individual. The effect of this action is that each property individual is asserted as a *roleAssertion* associating the property to the concept individual, and the new concept individual is marked as *created*. At this point it should be stated that when dealing with concept intersection, it is required to create the exact type. Let $A \sqsubseteq B \sqcap D$, creating an individual of type B and D is interpreted as two separate individuals, and thus not an instance of A. To create an instance of type A, it has to be created explicitly. On the other hand, creating an element of type A will have all properties associated with B and D.

$$
\begin{aligned}
\texttt{Operator} &= \mathit{createConcept}(c : t_C, [p_1 : P_1, \ldots, p_n : P_n]) \\
\texttt{pre} &= \neg \mathit{created}(c) \wedge \mathit{created}(p_1) \wedge \cdots \wedge \mathit{created}(p_n) \wedge \\
&\quad \neg \exists i_1 : \mathit{individual}, a_1 : \mathit{roleAssertion} \\
&\qquad (\mathit{domain}(a_1, i_1) \wedge \mathit{role}(a_1, \mathit{role}_{p_1}) \wedge \mathit{range}(a_1, p_1) \wedge \mathit{asserted}(a_1)) \wedge \\
&\quad \exists i_1 : \mathit{individual}, a_1 : \mathit{roleAssertion} \\
&\qquad (\mathit{domain}(a_1, i_1) \wedge \mathit{role}(a_1, \mathit{role}_{p_1}) \wedge \mathit{range}(a_1, p_1)) \wedge \\
&\quad \ldots \\
&\quad \neg \exists i_n : \mathit{individual}, a_n : \mathit{roleAssertion} \\
&\qquad (\mathit{domain}(a_n, i_n) \wedge \mathit{role}(a_n, \mathit{role}_{p_n}) \wedge \mathit{range}(a_n, p_n) \wedge \mathit{asserted}(a_n)) \wedge \\
&\quad \exists i_n : \mathit{individual}, a_n : \mathit{roleAssertion} \\
&\qquad (\mathit{domain}(a_n, i_n) \wedge \mathit{role}(a_n, \mathit{role}_{p_n}) \wedge \mathit{range}(a_n, p_n)) \\
\texttt{eff} &= \mathit{created}(c) \wedge \\
&\quad \forall a_1 : \mathit{roleAssertion} \\
&\qquad ((\mathit{domain}(a_1, c) \wedge \mathit{role}(a_1, \mathit{role}_{p_1}) \wedge \mathit{range}(a_1, p_1)) \rhd \mathit{asserted}(a_1)) \wedge \\
&\quad \ldots \\
&\quad \forall a_n : \mathit{roleAssertion} \\
&\qquad ((\mathit{domain}(a_n, c) \wedge \mathit{role}(a_n, \mathit{role}_{p_n}) \wedge \mathit{range}(a_n, p_n)) \rhd \mathit{asserted}(a_n))
\end{aligned}
$$

Here, role_{p_n} is the role associated with the property p_n, t_C the type of the concept C, and $P_1, \ldots P_n$ are the types of the properties. In the *precondition* section it is first ensured that there are no assertions with the passed parameter and any other individual or role, which is already marked as asserted. This ensures that the concrete property has not yet been used. Secondly the existence of such a *roleAssertion* is checked. This guarantees that the effect of the action can later mark the *roleAssertion* as asserted.

5.2 Creating the Planning Task

This section will discuss how the planning problem can be generated from the target assertion and the ontology. Starting from the target assertion, all related concepts, roles, and properties are identified. For each of these identified elements, a corresponding object (representing an individual of that type) is added to the set of task-dependent constants and initialized in the initial state s_0. We can see now that all concepts are treated as domain-dependent constants, and individuals are treated as task-dependent constants. Planning objects for all elements required for the target assertion together with all its related elements (properties, roles, concepts) are then initialized in s_0 by associating the properties to their respective concept instance. This is achieved by adding the corresponding *roleAssertions* to s_0.

Similarly the roles are constructed by adding objects for domain, range, and role assertion to the planning task, and initialising them in s_0, whereby existing range or domain objects must be taken in to account. This is achieved by creating unique identifiers for each object. By doing this for all concepts, roles, and properties encountered during the identification of related elements of the target assertion, we ensure that in the goal state $s_\star$ all objects will have been created or asserted, ensuring that the newly asserted knowledge holds even under the closed-world assumption.

If the target assertion was defined as being a concept assertion, then we add this assertion to the goal description of the problem as $\mathit{created}(a_0)$, equally, if the target assertion was a role assertion, then we add it to the goal state as $\mathit{asserted}(a_0)$.

An Example Plan. Consider again the very simple ontology from Figure 1 and the goal of annotating a person as an author of a book. The target assertion would then be $(\mathit{person1}, \mathit{book1}) : \mathit{isAuthor}$ for arbitrary but fixed individuals *person1* of type *Person* and *book1* of type *Book*. Executing our tool as described above would identify *Person*, *name*, *Book*, and *title* as relevant elements, and require $(\mathit{person1}, \mathit{book1}) : \mathit{isAuthor}$ to be asserted in the goal state. Four individuals would be generated in the initial state of the problem, which the planner would try to set as *created*. These individuals would be a *Person*, a *Book*, a *title*, and a *name*. Additionally, three role assertions would be generated mapping the *name* and *title* to the respective elements, and one for the target assertion $(\mathit{person1}, \mathit{book1}) : \mathit{isAuthor}$. A resulting plan would be as follows:

```
createname unknownname
create person1 unknownname
createtitle unknowntitle
createbook book1 unknowntitle
assertRole person1 isauthor book1
```

This plan can be interpreted as:

1. Create a Person *person1* with the name `unknownname`.
2. Create a Book *book1* with the title `unknowntitle`.
3. Define *person1* as author of *book1*.

6 From Plan to Workflow

A plan for the planning task resulting from our translation is a sequence of *create* and *assert* statements. These can be used to define the steps in a workflow. Each *create* step either creates a concept instance or a property. The *create* actions of properties can be interpreted as user input. Therefore the concept instance creation steps can be grouped together with their respective property creations to create a single workflow step. Due to the fact that all objects (concept instances and properties) are created prior to their usage, *assert* actions can be executed without further user input, and can be treated as separate workflow step. These *assert* steps will usually then be executed automatically, but depending on the application might be triggered manually.

Workflow Definition. Many ways exist for formal definition of workflows, among them the XML Process Definition Language(XPDL) [19], and the Business Process Model and Notation (BPMN) [17]. Since the requirements of the data management system in development were very limited, a very lightweight workflow definition was developed. This simple system consists of steps to be executed in a linear workflow. For the workflow to be executed on multiple applications, a JSON encoding was chosen. Each step is hereby defined by a list of actions to be taken and a list of resulting ontology assertions. The sequence in which these steps need to be taken is encoded by a simple enumeration. For the addition of branching in the workflow, a list of follow-up steps may be added to each step, hereby replacing the simple numbering by unique identifiers.

7 Adding Nondeterministic Actions

In this section we will shortly discuss how the above ideas can be extended to provide the required nondeterminism, which is introduced by user interaction. In the simplest form this can be interpreted as the user being presented with two options for creating the same object. Let us say the user is supposed to state the author of a book. This can be achieved by selecting a person from a list of existing persons, or, if the required person is not on the list, by adding a new person to the ontology. In this case we have to model our *create* actions as nondeterministic actions, which instead of a single effect, have a set of possible effects. For each possible outcome of the action, a different plan has to be generated. This has the consequence that instead of an ordered list of assertions, we are presented with a tree of actions, with each action having multiple successors.

Such a tree or DAG structure that solves a planning task no matter which action outcomes take place is called a *strong plan* [6]. Notice that we really require *strong* plans, which are only allowed to branch, as opposed to *strong cyclic* plans, which are also allowed to have loops, in our scenario. Finding strong plans essentially boils down to AND/OR graph search, for which there are various approaches, including symbolic backward search as used by the MBP planner [6], informed forward search as used by CONTINGENT-FF [11] and MYND [14], and offline replanning with generalization of subplans as successfully proposed as part of the PRP planner [15]. Here, we will not go into the details of these algorithms and planners, but rather point out that we can choose any such approach and use it as a black box to obtain a solution. Integration into our framework is considered future work.

8 Preliminary Results

In this paper, we showed that AI planning is suitable for generating workflows for managing knowledge stored and modelled in an ontology. During the development of this paper, multiple ontologies where designed for testing, including the ontology used in our archival system. During our experiments we were able to fully automatically generate the workflow for asserting a new individual comprising of 20 data properties, 12 roles and 13 related concept instances into our test ontology. The resulting workflows generated showed great promise for real-world application. Given an ontology O, we were able to generate an ordered list of assertions achieving the target assertion, by translating the ontology and the target assertion into a planning task Π, finding a plan π for Π, and converting this plan back to a workflow achieving the target assertion.

9 Future Work

As mentioned earlier, we would like to extend this work to a more expressive description logic supporting full $\mathcal{ALF}$ functionality. The main issue here will be identifying the preconditions and effects of the *create* and *assert* actions. Additionally to adding more functionality on the ontology side, migrating to a more widely used and expressive workflow modelling language such as XPDL or BPMN would increase the usability in more general scenarios.

In real-world applications, workflows are often executed by multiple agents, with each agent having certain rights to execute parts of the workflow. Adding this to our system could be achieved by implementing this in a multi-agent planning scenario, with each agent having only the actions available, which the corresponding real-world agent would have the rights to execute.

Large-scale applications will usually have workflows that can be split into multiple smaller ones, which might be executed multiple times (by multiple agents). For this, sub-workflow detection needs to be executed, identifying workflows-sections common to multiple different workflows, and extracting these, so they can be reused multiple times.

10 Acknowledgements

This work has partly been supported by the German Research Foundation under grant EXC 1086.

References

1. Baader, F., Nutt, W.: Basic description logics. In: Baader, F., Calvanese, D., McGuinness, D., Nardi, D., Patel-Schneider, P. (eds.) The Description Logic Handbook, chap. 2, pp. 43–96. Cambridge University Press (2003)
2. Bäckström, C., Nebel, B.: Complexity results for SAS+ planning. Computational Intelligence 11, 625–656 (1995)

3. Bertoli, P., Pistore, M., Traverso, P.: Automated composition of web services via planning in asynchronous domains. Artificial Intelligence 174(3–4), 316–361 (2010)
4. Bouillet, E., Feblowitz, M., Liu, Z., Ranganathan, A., Riabov, A.: A knowledge engineering and planning framework based on owl ontologies. Proceedings of the Second International Competition on Knowledge Engineering (2007)
5. Calvanese, D., Montali, M., Patrizi, F., Stawowy, M.: Plan synthesis for knowledge and action bases. In: Proc. of the 25th Int. Joint Conf. on Artificial Intelligence (IJCAI 2016). AAAI Press (2016), to appear
6. Cimatti, A., Pistore, M., Roveri, M., Traverso, P.: Weak, strong, and strong cyclic planning via symbolic model checking. Artificial Intelligence 147(1–2), 35–84 (2003)
7. Dublin Core Metadata Initiative: Dublin Core (April 2016), `http://http://dublincore.org/`
8. Fikes, R.E., Nilsson, N.J.: STRIPS: A new approach to the application of theorem proving to problem solving. Artificial Intelligence 2(3), 189–208 (1971)
9. Geffner, H., Bonet, B.: A Concise Introduction to Models and Methods for Automated Planning (2013)
10. Helmert, M.: The fast downward planning system. Journal of Artificial Intelligence Research (JAIR) 26, 191–246 (2006)
11. Hoffmann, J., Brafman, R.: Contingent planning via heuristic forward search with implicit belief states. In: Proc. 15th International Conference on Automated Planning and Scheduling (ICAPS 2005). pp. 71–80 (2005)
12. Hoffmann, J., Weber, I., Kraft, F.M.: SAP Speaks PDDL: Exploiting a Software-Engineering Model for Planning in Business Process Management. Journal of Artificial Intelligence Research 44, 587–632 (2012)
13. Lenzerini, M.: Ontology-based data management. In: Proceedings of the 20th ACM International Conference on Information and Knowledge Management. pp. 5–6. CIKM '11, ACM, New York, NY, USA (2011), `http://doi.acm.org/10.1145/2063576.2063582`
14. Mattmüller, R., Ortlieb, M., Helmert, M., Bercher, P.: Pattern database heuristics for fully observable nondeterministic planning. In: Proc. 20th International Conference on Automated Planning and Scheduling (ICAPS 2010). pp. 105–112 (2010)
15. Muise, C., McIlraith, S.A., Beck, J.C.: Improved non-deterministic planning by exploiting state relevance. In: Proc. 22nd International Conference on Automated Planning and Scheduling (ICAPS 2012) (2012)
16. Nau, D., Ghallab, M., Traverso, P.: Automated Planning: Theory & Practice (2004)
17. Object Management Group: Business Process Model And Notation^{TM}(BPMN^{TM}) (April 2016), `http://www.omg.org/spec/BPMN/`
18. Pednault, E.: ADL: Exploring the middle ground between STRIPS and the situation calculus. In: Proc. 1st International Conference on Principles of Knowledge Representation and Reasoning (KR 1989). pp. 324–332 (1989)
19. Workflow Management Coalition: XPLD (April 2016), `http://www.xpdl.org/`

Transforming Complex Business Challenges into Opportunities for Innovative Change - An Application for Planning and Scheduling Technology

Brian Drabble
DMM Ventures, Inc
Yorktown, United States

Bernd Schattenberg
Büro für intelligente Technologie-Beratung
Laupheim, Germany

Abstract

The new driving force of today's market has many names. Some call it Digitalization, Internet of Things, Industry 4.0, and many more. Based on technological advancements, the impact on the physical world with actionable information technology has been pushed to new levels. This in turn enabled small and agile players to create so-called disruptive innovations and to increase pressure on established players. As a consequence, all industries face a tremendous change. Both established as well as new players thus face a constantly growing complexity. Traditional decision support systems, which focus on the operational level, turn out to be ineffective to address that complexity. Additionally, businesses and organizations are facing new challenges such as the issues associated with the "Circular Economy" and the implications it has for the way they conduct their businesses. This presentation gives an introduction to application domains in this realm and points out solutions to current industries' most pressing issues, in which Artificial Intelligence Planning and Scheduling technology plays a central role.

Introduction – The Age of Digitization

Over recent years, the *digitization* wave mutated into a substantial challenge for enterprises of any size. What started out as a notion of "utilizing information technology" became one of the central driving forces in today's markets. The speed and versatility of the digital economy increases the pressure on virtually every traditional industry and service provider. The main aspects of this phenomenon are coined by Clayton M. Christensen by the term *disruptive innovations*, which basically means that there exist innovations, that create new markets and value networks, effectively displacing the players in existing markets (Bower and Christensen 1995). With the rise of the digital economy, the frequency and amplitude of such disruptive changes has increased immensely. In addition, recent economic developments like Circular Economy (CE) with its integral causal feedback loops represents an economical challenge but none the less a reasonable business opportunity (Ellen MacArthur Foundation 2015). Furthermore, it is an excellent use case for Artificial Intelligence Planning and Scheduling (AI P&S) technology, because strategic decisions in CE are inherently more complex than traditional ones.

Submitted to the 30th Workshop "Planen/Scheduling und Konfigurieren/Entwerfen" (PuK), Klagenfurt, Austria, September 26, 2016.

In summary, we nowadays find disruptiveness as the architect of new business models. This implies for especially large players the need to adapt faster and with increasingly substantial change to stay synchronized with market dynamics (Kagermann 2015). Organizational scale, which was the former guarantor for success, now turns into a big disadvantage. Without having appropriate support at the operational level as well as at the strategic level we will see more organizations being displaced from the market.

The classical digitization strategies of major companies, like the closely related initiatives "Industry 4.0" and "Internet of Things" do on a broader scale, heavily focus on the technical issues of collaboration on the operational level. Hence, they focus on solutions to interoperability- and infrastructure-related problems together with the respective standards for their implementation. This represents a traditional, mostly on complication focused approach. Implications arising from complexity are not sufficiently covered by these approaches, as they do not take into account the dynamics of the processes involved and organizational entities that are required to explore upcoming market opportunities.

In order to address these business challenges in a constructive manner, we propose a paradigm that follows a goal-driven approach: First, the involved stakeholders agree on a (potentially new) value proposition and corresponding business models. Then they assess their existing processes, their own capabilities, and that of potential collaborators. From this information they develop the steps necessary to deliver that value proposition and the structure of the value-added chain that implements the desired business model – and they do so with support by AI P&S technology. In short: driven by the goal of serving a new market or delivering an innovative product, the stakeholders employ planning models and algorithms to decide how to realize their goals with the assistance of whom in which way. Since all these business dynamics are basically goal-oriented, the AI P&S community's technology portfolio constitutes a perfect match for the implicitly present demand.

We believe that – at this point of the economic development – the proposed AI P&S approach is considerably more adequate for the digital age than other paradigms, in particular manual planning techniques. How exactly AI P&S fits into the picture of the digitization and disruption movements portrayed above will be motivated in the following sections.

Transformation: Business Challenges Can Become Opportunities for Innovation

We begin with some reflections on the characteristics of the problems that we face when implementing a digitization-induced change in an organization. To this end, we can make the following four observations:

1. Every business is defined by its business model and a corresponding value-added chain. Every link of that chain, that means, every compartment of the company like *production* or *marketing*, is governed in terms of its workflows by well-defined business processes.
2. In general, these business processes are locally both well understood and highly optimized. This is, however, usually not the case for the implicit dependencies and causalities (or so-called *n-order effects*) on the level of a global value-added chain.
3. Established and, in particular, large businesses have set-up a highly specialized and efficient, workflows. However, these huge organiztions are usually inflexible which hampers their process change efforts. They become increasingly mandatory in cooperation and CE scenarios. This makes them particularly reluctant to adopting new *business strategies*. In addition, it renders them unable to react to disruptive stimuli in an adequate manner, because change in the organization has to propagate up the structural hierarchies and back. Adapting established business processes is only possible as a long-term initiative with numerous occasions being reported of failed company mergers.
4. Small businesses, for example start-up firms, do work completely different for that matter. Thus, cooperating with another business of similar size – whether within the same market segment and technology strain or not – is typically "only one phone-call away". All business models and value-added chains are explicitly known to the stakeholders and usually negotiable. Joint ventures are born by integrating individual contributions to a joint value proposition.

As stated above, economic scale was the key attribute to grant access to high volumes and possibly margins. Organizations therefore are structured around the idea of setting up static value chains to orchestrate actions of a large set of stakeholders. Functional decomposition together with low level of vertical integration resulted in inflexible structures. Change, in any form, is risk and will be impacted from both the chain and the involved functions.

A solution to this problem needs to ensure both alignment, to address efficiency, and to allow for autonomy, to address upcoming changes. Statically defined structures, processes and technologies won't be able to do this job. Our proposed goal-based approach ensures a convergent and aligned value chain that can instantaneously implement required opportunistic local transformation impulses. Required actions are developed and compliance is sustained by AI P&S and are integrated directly in to day-to-day operations.

The key strategic element of our proposed effective business decision support is to facilitate "controlled flexibility", that means, flexibly setting up alliances with business partners in order to realize new products and value propositions that were not possible by the individual firms alone. But this means instead of cooperating on a purely operational level, cooperations have to be installed on the organizational level, too. With an adequately detailed model of the stakeholders' value-added chains and business processes, AI P&S is able to produce plans that reflect:

1. Ad-hoc alignment of strategic goals, that means, cooperating in a trans-organizational way along the horizontal value-added chain. Improved products at considerably lower overhead costs make this scenario commercially interesting even for smaller markets.
2. Ad-hoc assignment of tasks, that is, utilizing new opportunities by creating and optimizing processes along the vertical value-added chain. This basically means, that the company can establish new processes and behaviors by utilizing its internal resources.

AI P&S is thereby employed to facilitate running dynamic organizations by designing aligned autonomous stakeholders. Eventually, both of the above notions of plans have to be utilized in order to gain the full benefit of the methodology and they work on both the large and the small scale:

- Setting up virtual organizations from the functional and organizational cells of the stakeholders' organizations. This can also be viewed as an implementation of important aspects of the *Rule of 150* (Gladwell 2006) and *Agile project management* (Highsmith 2009) in that planning conceptually takes defined organizational structures as a source for re-groupings in view of a new purpose.
- Controlling and orchestrating technical systems inside businesses. This domain has been studied for some time by the planning community, among others under the aspects of scheduling, mission-planning, and multi-agency. Although it resembles the application area of classical business process models (BPM), these processes are highly dynamic in nature and are most certainly never executed on a regular basis. Many techniques from the BPM literature will therefore not be available in this setting.

It becomes clear that, on a global, organization-wide scale, more than one technology is needed. A comprehensive and universal approach has to address collaboration issues and the differences of industry-specific applications at basically every single level of detail and ranging from an initial knowledge acquisition phase to the final process monitoring. Currently, the economy almost exclusively demands for information processing methods to harvest implicit information from inside their own business and from their (potential) customers. Techniques including data analytics and data mining provide access to this information and provide it in a form that can be directly used by AI P&S technologies. This raises another dimension of complexity to this problem, namely, what to do with all this knowledge [1]. We note that most of the relevant knowledge concerning the stakeholders strategic and operational options (viz., the very knowledge required for effectively employing AI P&S methods as sketched above) is available though is often overlooked in current approaches to AI P&S.

By adopting a more pragmatic approach, we therefore suggest concentrating on the first part of the overall scenario in order to establish AI P&S methods as our customers' primary means to manage and operationalize knowledge about their business dynamics. From that, future support methods can emerge, which integrate more stages of a comprehensive issue treatment approach and that introduce new facets for specific market situations, organization types, and so forth.

Our first application domain isolates an issue of the manufacturing systems engineering industry, which faces a significant change in their business model, namely the problem of responding to batch size 1 requests. requests. While we have used the batch 1 as an illustrative example, the same type of goal and plan driven approach applies to design, analysis and issues of the circuar economy. That means, their customers become increasingly interested in individualized products and therefore order custom-made units. Currently, established procedures are tailored for mass-production, so our proposed paradigm will make a difference by applying planning to an on-demand setup of production workflows, production resources, and proper handshakes with subcontractors, external suppliers, and internal service providers.

Two key components of one such solution are specific instances of AI P&S technology, deployed following in the Software-as-a-Service paradigm. The next section gives some details for these two aspects.

Adequate System Support for Transformations

Artificial Intelligence Planning and Scheduling Technology

In recent years, an increasing demand for more personalized products finally reached those industries which provide the actual product makers with their production tools; among them, the manufacturing systems engineering industry. These companies face the problem of receiving a decreasing number of large quantity orders, say, for supplying a manufacturing plant with dozens of virtually identical machines, and instead getting more and more orders for single, custom-tailored machines. Their evolutionary balanced business models begin to suffer for mainly two reasons:

1. Re-configuring the factory site such that the order can be processed is inherently costly, because it has been set-up in structurally fixed ways. And in addition, with every product being typically processed through a large number of passes on an equally large number of work stations, any deviation from an established routine challenges the organization's productivity.
2. Established batch processes are inadequate and have to be re-designed into more project-oriented *bidireactional* interactions that coordinate all in-house as well as subcontracted stakeholders like order processing, purchasing department, construction/production of components, sales department, and so forth.

Both factors are mutually amplified up to the point where nowadays the entrepreneurial risk becomes vital.

We propose the employment of *hybrid planning* (Schattenberg 2009; Kambhampati, Mali, and Srivastava 1998; Castillo, Fernández-Olivares, and González 2000) in these scenarios. This paradigm integrates building plans based on the individual action's causal structure (also referred to as *partial-order causal-link planning* (Penberthy and Weld 1992; McAllester and Rosenblitt 1991)) with obtaining plans from iteratively implementing abstract actions by pre-defined partial solutions (the so-called *hierarchical task-network planning* (Erol, Hendler, and Nau 1994; Yang 1998)). The hierarchical domain model aspects thereby represent regular solutions provided by domain experts, while the causality-based techniques complete underspecified procedures and address exceptional cases. Although any state-based approaches may be used in application areas of this kind (Rodríguez-Moreno et al. 2007; Hoffmann, Weber, and Kraft 2012), we prefer the hybrid methodology for their ability to adequately reflect procedural knowledge in combination with addressing variance by reasoning from first principles. As described above, the situation for the stakeholders maps onto the hybrid modeling method as follows:

- State of the art procedures are key to the industrial businesses. Back in the days, when running a business was just *complicated*, the stakeholders figured out very effectively all relevant processes and how to implement them. In terms of hybrid planning, the procedures are mapped on task networks, which are basically plans, consisting of tasks as process steps, orderings between the tasks, and causal dependencies between them. The procedures can be organized in a hierarchical fashion, such that different process variants can be subsumed as a set of tasks networks that *implement* an abstract place-holder task or process step, which may in turn be part of some more abstract process specifications, and so on. The emerging hierarchy of processes/tasks reflects the organizations' options on the strategic level (abstract tasks) as well as on the operational (primitive tasks).
- Solid processes may be key, but they are for stable organizations only. As long as a complicated situation is coped with by effective routines, everything is fine. But at some point the size-dimension of organizations has been surpassed by the dimension of their structural dependencies and thus turned business into *complex* ventures. In most real-world situations, the procedures will be underspecified and plainly not applicable anymore in any change situation. This is where causal reasoning on the task level, primitive or abstract, comes into play. By applying a means-end analysis and proving causal interactions and dependencies, planning builds goal-specific

[1] c.f. Quentin Hardy, "The Peril of Knowledge Everywhere", The New York Times, May 10, 2014

sequences of tasks and processes that implement proper workflows across organization boundaries, if required.

The adequacy of the hybrid planning technology and its domain modeling formalisms has been proven in similar application domains (Estlin, Chien, and Wang 1997; Castillo, Fernández-Olivares, and González 2001). We also note that capturing the (planning) models that represent their organizations and options is already an extremely valuable information for the stakeholders, for this knowledge most often lies unused or is not available in a sufficiently formal and, hence, unambiguous format.

While scheduling can already be found in numerous commercial application scenarios, ranging from staffing (Stylianou, Gerasimou, and Andreou 2012) to manufacturing scheduling (Framinan, Leisten, and García 2014), it becomes necessary in this wider sense to integrate planning and scheduling on basically every abstraction level of the model. Obviously, resource reasoning is relevant to all economic problems, but in the transformation scenario not all of the valid action options are known in advance. We learn that optimization issues in ad-hoc alliances are of lower-ranking interest (these will be addressed later when the cooperations are more consolidated), but a reliable feasibility analysis is most definitely vital.

Last, but not least, some additional aspects become important when the solution is to be fielded successfully, namely plan repair, interactive planning, and plan explanation (Schattenberg 2015). These functionalities are requested by practical considerations, because in particular at this early stage, all domain models and mutual understandings about the solution spaces are at any point in time still "work in progress". Recovering from not customer-approved solutions as well as guiding search more or less directly by domain experts is the economically most efficient way to begin with. On the other hand, if solutions are to be presented to decision-makers, the solution has to be trusted and finally accepted as the verdict of a virtual expert. This becomes in particular an issue when stakeholders from different organizations and backgrounds/disciplines meet.

Supporting Solution Generation with a Platform Strategy

A monolithic approach, in which domain management, AI P&S execution and human interaction management is integrated into a single software artifact turned out to be overly restrictive and not well suited to explore the arising market opportunities as outlined above. Our proposed architecture is based on loosely coupled micro services. The overall system can be decomposed into these four building blocks:

1. *Domain modeling and management*, that is a collection of tools to store, version, and collaborate on domain models. In our case we make use of text file based representations of domains, including PDDL [2].

   The PDDL representation is augmented and fused with a dependency network based model (Drabble 2014). This adopts a "system of systems" approach to domain modelling allowing for direct, indirect, cascading and cumulative effects of actions to be represented and reasoned with. A dependency network model consists of nodes (persons, groups, organizations, resources, locations, concepts, etc.) with pairs of nodes linked by arcs. The arcs specify strength of the dependency (range 1 – 10) and the nature of the dependency (actor operates physical, physical supplies physical, etc.). These direct dependencies are used to calculate transitive dependency scores for each node in the network. These scores are then ranked to identify the most important nodes in network. The ranking provides a user with the ability to identify bottlenecks (over dependency on a specified node), lack of robustness and opportunities for network function and output improvement. These identified improvements are used to generate goals and tasks from which intelligent tools can generate appropriate plans and schedules. Plans are converted into additional nodes and links which are added to the dependency network. These additional links and nodes may identify new dependencies or increase the score of known dependencies. This allows users to identify weaknesses in their plans and to iteratively improve them over time.

   As the creation and maintenance of domains is a highly iterative and collaborative process, providing the conceptual guidance during the complete lifecycle of the application, we went for the integration of GitHub as one of the widely supported and verified collaboration platforms (Longo and Kelley 2015). Versioning, branching, and pull-request support helps us to streamline the whole process and it is closely related to established technologies and development workflows.

2. *Plan execution*, that is specifically a question of which AI P&S strategy and philosophy is best suited to solve a certain problem. We found that there is a great demand for pluggable architectures, because application domains and therewith the effectiveness of AI P&S technology varies. Our planning as a service platform makes use of the Docker virtualization infrastructure, in which planner *configurations* are available as reusable components (Anderson 2015). They are immutable and versioned, such that at every time point any previously available image can be incorporated. Standardization helps to use commercial off-the-shelf cloud service instances to run these components at reasonable cost and with almost linear horizontal scaling support.

3. *Human interaction management*, that is a standardized way for humans to interact with the specific AI P&S setup that is prepared for a given application. We consider both development and maintenance as well as in-process interaction as use cases for our application front-end. The front-end is implemented as a state-of-the-art web interface. We integrate the pieces of our micro-service archi-

[2] In its latest version 3.1, the Planning Domain Definition Language does not support hierarchical domain model aspects. For those application scenarios in which non-hierarchical planning suffices, we propose planning systems that comply with the standard summarized in Daniel L. Kovacs' BNF description. In most cases, however, we employ a proprietary hybrid modeling language.

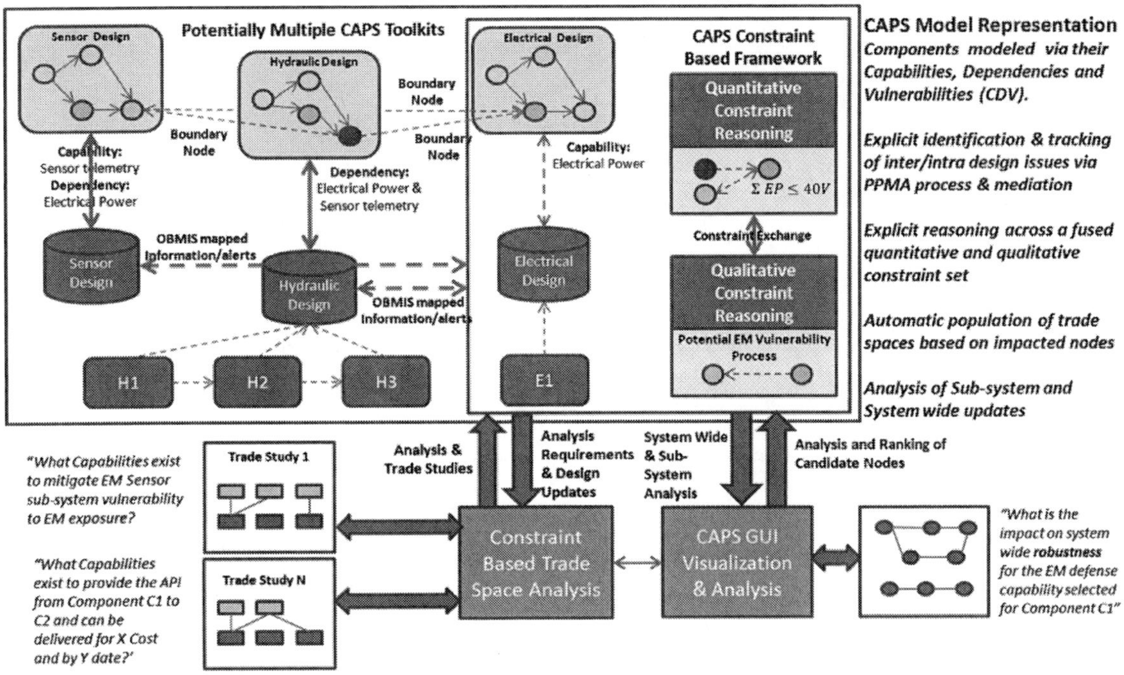

Figure 1: Cassandra Analysis and Planning System (CAPS) Architecture Overview

tecture into a seamless user experience. The main use cases are (1) environment configuration and maintenance, (2) tracking of the plan generation processes, (3) historical results archive, (4) error tracking and monitoring, and (5) simple human-machine interactions.

4. *Application Programming Interface (API)*, that is a machine-to-machine interface for sensors and actors of the application domain to directly interact with the AI P&S platform. We support both design/maintenance and operational use-cases. On the one hand, for example, a simple command line utility can be used by domain architects to trigger and monitor planning processes from a local copy of the domain repository whereas on the other hand a process execution support system can trigger and consume the results of the plan and schedule generation based on current sensor data and references to existing domains.

The dependency model described earlier was used as the primary representation for the CAPS (Drabble 2015). CAPS provides a distributed collaborative design and planning toolkit which allows individual designers to see the consequences of their own decisions and the impacts on other dependent designs. An overview of the CAPS system is provided in Figure 1 which shows the basic components of the architecture.

The right side of Figure 1 shows an instantiation of CAPS to support an EP sub-system designer and comprises the GUI through which the designer can view their design as a dependency graph, the information sources (for example, manuals, documents, specifications, etc.) the designers is using and details of the design held in the quantitative and qualitative systems respectively. This allows the EP designer to "drill down" on design nodes in the GUI to identify what options are available for a node (component or subsystem), instigate a trade study, assess the effects on their design of a decision they are considering, prioritize design decisions based on the effect on the design, etc. The Trade Space analysis component allows the EP designer to instigate trade studies which are auto-populated by CAPS based on the capability, dependency and vulnerability (CDV) of the node(s) selected by the designer. For example, the dependency of a hydraulic sensor on EP identifies it as a node potentially impacted by the trade study, the capability of generators to output different amounts of EP identifies them as candidates and the potential vulnerability of one or more of the impacted sensors to EM radiation also makes them a candidate. This allows CAPS to rank potential node decomposition and/or instantiations based on how well their capabilities meet the overall specification, their impact on other open decisions and identify potential trade-offs. For example, the choice of a generator in the EP sub-system design which has a slightly higher EM output than the "cheapest cost" choice would avoid imposing a "single choice" option on several components in the hydraulic sub-system design. The automatic population of the trade study matrix and identification of trade-offs firstly ensures only available options are considered, secondly it frees the user from having to search for trade-off options and thirdly decreases the overall design time by only requiring designers to interact when the mitigation step in the Propose $\rightarrow$ Propogate $\rightarrow$ Mediate $\rightarrow$ Assert process cannot find a suitable set of trade-offs.

Having this integrative platform in place is a key asset to focus on the development of specific AI P&S technologies whilst ensuring that domain architects can focus on their work. With emerging interoperable domain languages the platform will be key to further speed up development and value creation of AI P&S technology in domains as stated above.

Conclusion

Artificial Intelligence Planning and Scheduling technology turns out to be a key resource to solve essential transformational challenges in the context of the ongoing digitization. However, it has to be understood more as a tool or capability than as an actual product. As a powerful capability, it fosters the ability of organizations to integrate new knowledge into their operational perspective more quickly and more safely. As a product, if you will, it delivers advice in form of actionable and valid plans.

At the end of our presentation we have to note, that the actual degree of automation depends on the actual business case. While some organization might be able to utilize fully automated transformation processes and workflows, others will benefit exclusively from cooperation and interaction plans in a negotiation-safe format. The proposed methodology is able to address any scenario within this spectrum at basically any level of abstraction. The described challenge of "batch size 1" to the manufacturing industry serves as an example for an instantiation of the AI P&S methodology in this domain.

Our vision can be summarized as follows: Like database systems sustained the scale of information that came with the growth of businesses and web/cloud technology sustained the scatterdness of that information in increasingly distribution organizations, so will AI P&S sustain the complexity of (re-) acting within huge organizational bodies. Eventually, it will be perceived as an integral layer in the technology stack of modern software products. In order to foster this development, future work will focus on making the technology an Open-Source movement, including comprehensive repositories of domain models; this will help to pick up the momentum by early adopters.

Acknowledgement

We would like to thank Jan-Jakob Wachs of *Bapo UG* and Markus Kuhnt of *disrupt consulting e.G.* for their valuable input and support in an earlier version of this paper.

References

[Anderson 2015] Anderson, C. 2015. Docker [software engineering]. *IEEE Software* 32(3):102–c3. doi:10.1109/MS.2015.62.

[Bower and Christensen 1995] Bower, J. L., and Christensen, C. M. 1995. Disruptive technologies: Catching the wave. *Harvard Business Review* 73(1):43–53.

[Castillo, Fernández-Olivares, and González 2000] Castillo, L. A.; Fernández-Olivares, J.; and González, A. 2000. A hybrid hierarchical/operator-based planning approach for the design of control programs. In *ECAI Workshop on Planning and Configuration: New results in planning, scheduling and design*, 1–10.

[Castillo, Fernández-Olivares, and González 2001] Castillo, L. A.; Fernández-Olivares, J.; and González, A. 2001. On the adequacy of hierarchical planning characteristics for real-world problem solving. In *Proceedings of VI European Conference of Planning*.

[Drabble 2014] Drabble, B. 2014. Modeling c2 networks as dependencies: Understanding what the real issues are. In Grant, T.; Janssen, R.; and Monsuur, H., eds., *Network Topology in Command and Control: Organization, Operation, and Evolution*. Hershey, PA: Information Science Reference. 125–151. doi:10.4018/978-1-4666-6058-8.ch006.

[Drabble 2015] Drabble, B. 2015. Dependency-based collaborative design: a comparison of modeling methods. *Journal of Concurrency and Computation: Practice and Experience*. John Wiley & Sons, Ltd, doi:10.1002/cpe.3445.

[Ellen MacArthur Foundation 2015] 2015. Towards a circular economy: Business rationale for an accelerated transition. Ellen MacArthur Foundation. https://www.ellenmacarthurfoundation.org.

[Erol, Hendler, and Nau 1994] Erol, K.; Hendler, J.; and Nau, D. S. 1994. UMCP: A sound and complete procedure for hierarchical task-network planning. In *Proceedings of the 2nd International Conference on Artificial Intelligence Planning Systems (AIPS 1994)*, 249–254.

[Estlin, Chien, and Wang 1997] Estlin, T. A.; Chien, S. A.; and Wang, X. 1997. An argument for a hybrid HTN/operator-based approach to planning. In *Proceedings of the 4th European Conference on Planning: Recent Advances in AI Planning*, 182–194.

[Framinan, Leisten, and García 2014] Framinan, J. M.; Leisten, R.; and García, R. R. 2014. *Manufacturing Scheduling Systems*. Springer London. doi:10.1007/978-1-4471-6272-8.

[Gladwell 2006] Gladwell, M. 2006. *The tipping point: How little things can make a big difference*. Little, Brown.

[Highsmith 2009] Highsmith, J. 2009. *Agile Project Management: Creating Innovative Products*. Agile Software Development Series. Pearson Education.

[Hoffmann, Weber, and Kraft 2012] Hoffmann, J.; Weber, I.; and Kraft, F. M. 2012. SAP speaks PDDL: exploiting a software-engineering model for planning in business process management. *J. Artif. Intell. Res. (JAIR)* 44:587–632. doi:10.1613/jair.3636.

[Kagermann 2015] Kagermann, H. 2015. Change through digitization—value creation in the age of industry 4.0. In Albach, H.; Meffert, H.; Pinkwart, A.; and Reichwald, R., eds., *Management of Permanent Change*. Springer Fachmedien Wiesbaden. 23–45. doi:10.1007/978-3-658-05014-6_2.

[Kambhampati, Mali, and Srivastava 1998] Kambhampati, S.; Mali, A.; and Srivastava, B. 1998. Hybrid planning for partially hierarchical domains. In *Proceedings of the 15th National Conference on Artificial Intelligence*, 882–888.

American Association for Artificial Intelligence (AAAI Press).

[Longo and Kelley 2015] Longo, J., and Kelley, T. M. 2015. Use of github as a platform for open collaboration on text documents. In *Proceedings of the 11th International Symposium on Open Collaboration*, OpenSym '15, 22:1–22:2. New York, NY, USA: ACM. doi:10.1145/2788993.2789838.

[McAllester and Rosenblitt 1991] McAllester, D., and Rosenblitt, D. 1991. Systematic nonlinear planning. In *Proceedings of the Ninth National Conference on Artificial Intelligence*, 634–639.

[Penberthy and Weld 1992] Penberthy, J. S., and Weld, D. S. 1992. UCPOP: A sound, complete, partial order planner for ADL. In *Proceedings of the third International Conference on Knowledge Representation and Reasoning*, 103–114.

[Rodríguez-Moreno et al. 2007] Rodríguez-Moreno, M. D.; Borrajo, D.; Cesta, A.; and Oddi, A. 2007. Integrating planning and scheduling in workflow domains. *Expert Systems with Applications* 33(2):389–406. http://dx.doi.org/10.1016/j.eswa.2006.05.027.

[Schattenberg 2009] Schattenberg, B. 2009. *Hybrid Planning And Scheduling*. Ph.D. Dissertation, Ulm University, Institute of Artificial Intelligence. urn:nbn:de:bsz:289-vts-68953.

[Schattenberg 2015] Schattenberg, B. 2015. Hybrid planning and scheduling. *KI - Künstliche Intelligenz*. Springer Berlin Heidelberg, doi:10.1007/s13218-015-0390-z.

[Stylianou, Gerasimou, and Andreou 2012] Stylianou, C.; Gerasimou, S.; and Andreou, A. 2012. A novel prototype tool for intelligent software project scheduling and staffing enhanced with personality factors. In *2012 IEEE 24th International Conference on Tools with Artificial Intelligence (ICTAI)*, volume 1, 277–284. doi:10.1109/ICTAI.2012.45.

[Yang 1998] Yang, Q. 1998. *Intelligent Planning. A Decomposition and Abstraction Based Approach*. Springer.

Declarative Decomposition and Dispatching for Large-Scale Job-Shop Scheduling*

Giacomo Da Col and Erich C. Teppan

Alpen-Adria-Universität Klagenfurt,
Universitätsstr. 65-67, 9020 Klagenfurt, Austria
{giacomo.da;erich.teppan}@aau.at

Abstract. Job-shop scheduling problems constitute a big challenge in nowadays industrial manufacturing environments. Because of the size of realistic problem instances, applied methods can only afford low computational costs. Furthermore, because of highly dynamic production regimes, adaptability is an absolute must. In state-of-the-art production factories the large-scale problem instances are split into subinstances, and greedy dispatching rules are applied to decide which job operation is to be loaded next on a machine. In this paper we propose a novel scheduling approach inspired by those hand-crafted scheduling routines. Our approach builds on problem decomposition for keeping computational costs low, dispatching rules for effectiveness and declarative programming for high adaptability and maintainability. We present first results proving the concept of our novel scheduling approach based on a new large-scale job-shop benchmark with proven optimal solutions.

Keywords: job-shop scheduling, problem decomposition, declarative programming

1 Introduction

The scheduling of jobs [6] is an important task in almost all production systems in order to optimize various objectives such as resource consumption, tardiness, or flow time. In general, jobs are structured into operations which must be allocated to resources such that various manufacturing constraints are satisfied and in addition an objective function is minimized. The job-shop scheduling problem (JSP) is among the most famous $\mathcal{NP}$-hard [12] and longest studied combinatorial problems (e.g. [4],). In this paper we focus on the makespan as the most classic optimization criterium. The makespan is the time needed for completing all job operations. Thus, the JSP can be defined as follows:

- Given is a set $M = \{1, \dots, m\}$ of machines and a set $J = \{1, \dots, j\}$ of jobs.

* The research for this paper was conducted in the scope of the project *Heuristic Intelligence (HINT)* in cooperation with Infineon Technologies Austria AG and Siemens AG Österreich funded by the Austrian research fund FFG under grant 840242. Authors are given in alphabetical order and contributed equally to this paper.

- Each job $j \in J$ consists of a sequence of operations $Ops_j = \{j_1, \ldots, j_{l_j}\}$ whereby j_{l_j} is the last operation of job j.
  Practically, jobs can be interpreted as products and operations can be interpreted as their production steps.
  With respect to a job j and its operation j_i (with $1 < i < l_j$), the operation j_{i+1} is called successor and the operation j_{i-1} is called predecessor.
- Each operation j_i has an operation length $length_{j_i} \in \mathbb{N}$.
- Each operation j_i is assigned to a machine $m_{j_i} \in M$ by which it is processed.
- A (consistent and complete) schedule consists of a starting time $start_{j_i}$ for each operation j_i such that:
  - An operation's successor starts after the operation has been finished, i.e. with respect to a job j and the operations j_i and j_{i+1}:
    - $start_{j_{i+1}} \geq start_{j_i} + length_{j_i}$
  - Operations processed by the same machine are non-overlapping, i.e. with respect to two operations $j_x \neq k_y$ with $m_{j_x} = m_{k_y}$:
    - $start_{j_x} \neq start_{k_y}$
    - $start_{j_x} < start_{k_y} \rightarrow start_{j_x} + length_{j_x} \leq start_{k_y}$
- Makespan, i.e. the time period needed for processing all operations, is minimized, i.e.:
  - $\max\limits_{j \in J, j_i \in Ops_j} \{start_{j_i} + length_{j_i}\} \rightarrow min$

The flexible job-shop scheduling problem (FJSP) is a variant of the JSP where for an operation there is a set of candidate machines that can process the operation, i.e. for each operation j_i there is a set $s_{j_i} \subseteq M$. Out of s_{j_i} there is one machine $m_{j_i} \in s_{j_i}$ which actually processes the operation. Hence, there is no predefined operation-to-machine assignment and the mapping of operations to machines is part of the problem.

In terms of complexity, the JSP is $\mathcal{NP}$-hard [11] and as it is a special case of the FJSP, also the FJSP is NP-hard. Thus, computing optimal solutions is only feasible for small problem instances.

Driven by the demands of the semiconductor industry, our general aim is the design of practically applicable algorithms for job-shop scheduling problems for domains comprising hundreds of machines and thousands of jobs and job operations. The size of such large-scale job-shop scheduling problem instances go beyond the usual benchmarks. For example, in the well-known job-shop benchmarks of [8] problem instances comprise not more than 50 jobs and 20 machines, i.e. the maximum branching factor in a corresponding search problem is 50.

In the case of our project partner Infineon Austria Technologies, common problem instances for a weekly workload are of the order of 10^4 operations on 10^2 machines in the back-end, i.e. where the products are made ready for shipping, and 10^5 operations on 10^3 machines in the front-end, i.e. where the chips are actually produced. The branching factors even go beyond the order of 10^3. On the one hand, this is due to the large number of jobs. On the other hand, this is because there are typically multiple machines equipped to perform a certain job operation, i.e. it is a flexible job-shop. Apparently, calculating optimal schedules for such large-scale problems are typically far out of reach for such domains.

State-of-the-art search algorithms for JSP and FJSP are local search methods like tabu search [17] or large-neighborhood search [19]. However, without equipping the search approaches with sophisticated domain specific heuristics the performance is quite limited [7, 1, 9]. Furthermore for large-scale problems, problem decomposition is absolutely needed [5]. When applying problem decomposition, a problem instance is partitioned into subinstances which are solved independently. The subsolutions are then combined again to form the overall solution.

Daily scheduling routines in semi-conductor factories like those of our project partner also build on problem decomposition on the one hand and heuristics on the other hand for producing scheduling solutions. The problem decomposition is hereby realized by partitioning the machines into so called workcenters. Each workcenter is responsible only for a fraction of operation types, i.e. job operations are assigned to workcenters rather than actual machines. The production plan is made for each workcenter independently based on dispatching rules, a widely employed state-of-the-art technique for dealing with large and complex scheduling problems in nowadays manufacturing environments [15].

Dispatching rules are greedy heuristics for step-wise deciding which is the operation to be processed next by a machine. Simple examples for dispatching rules are first-come-first-serve, i.e. the preference of the longest waiting operation, or shortest-job-first. One of the most effective dispatching rules for minimizing the makespan is the most-total-work-remaining (MTWR) rule [18]. According to MTWR, the next operation to be dispatched belongs to a job such that the sum of lengths of all remaining operations is maximal. One big advantage of dispatching rules is that they can be computed typically in linear time. Another big advantage is their flexibility. Dispatching rules can be changed, adapted or combined easily in order to react on changing order situations as well as changing product portfolios. This is crucial for modern manufacturing regimes like mass customization [10], just-in-time or lean production [16]. Moreover, almost every real-world scheduling problem has specific constraints regarding the manufacturing processes.

Consequently, in order to be successfully applied in real-life production environments, an approach for automatic decomposition and dispatching must be easily adaptable. In particular, it must be possible to implement different decomposition methods and dispatching rules in a compact but well-maintainable form.

One way of achieving high adaptability and maintainability is declarative programming. Declarative programming approaches such as answer set and constraint programming [13, 2] provide high-level language representation features. Encodings specify the problem to be solved rather than how it is to be solved, which leads to short and well-maintainable code. A general problem solver is then responsible for finding a consistent solution for the encoded problem. As a consequence, declarative approaches have already been often applied to scheduling problems (e.g. [3]). However, for large-scale problems, their direct applicability is limited. For example, incremental scheduling problem instances (a variant of FJSP) used in the answer set programming competition [1] do not comprise more than 120 job operations on max 7 machines. Also constraint programming approaches cannot be directly applied on problems like investigated in this paper. This is due to the fact that otherwise well-applicable global constraints [2] possess quadratic complexities which, in the light of instances comprising up to 10000 job operations and 100 machines, can already be too much.

In this paper we present a novel scheduling approach building on declarative programming in order to benefit from the high-level and compact knowledge representation and combine it with problem decomposition and dispatching rules in order to have the best of the different worlds: adaptability and extendability, low computational costs and effectiveness.

The remainder of the paper is structured as follows: In the next section we present a novel scheduling approach in which it is possible to program decomposition and scheduling rules by means of declarative programming. We describe the architecture and also a first prototype following this architecture. In Section 3 we describe a new large-scale benchmark of JSP and FJSP instances. The instances are patterned on scheduling problems of our project partner Infineon Austria Technologies and comprise up to more than 2000 jobs with up to more than 10000 operations in total to be scheduled on up to 100 machines. The new benchmark instances also have the feature of proven minimal makespans. In Section 4 we present first experimental results clearly proving the new concept. Section 5 concludes the paper.

2 A Novel Scheduling Approach

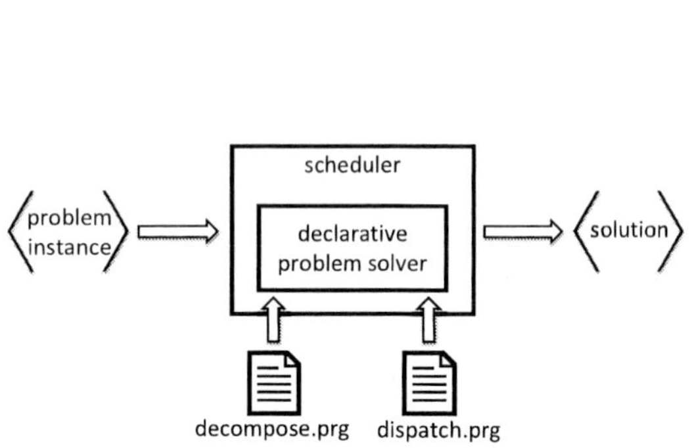

Fig. 1. General architecture of the scheduler

[1] https://www.mat.unical.it/aspcomp2014/

[2] http://sofdem.github.io/gccat/

Architecture Figure 1 shows the general architecture of our scheduling approach. Conforming to our proposed architecture, a scheduler is build upon a general purpose declarative problem solver. This can be - but is not limited to - constraint solvers like Gecode[3] or Jacop[4], answer set solvers like Clingo[5] or hybrids like proposed in [2, 14].

Two declarative programs written in the language of the solver are responsible to define the scheduling behavior. In particular, *decompose.prg* specifies the strategy for the problem decomposition, i.e. the method for splitting the problem instance into subinstances, which are then treated independently. How those subinstances are processed is determined by a dispatching rule defined in *dispatch.prg*.

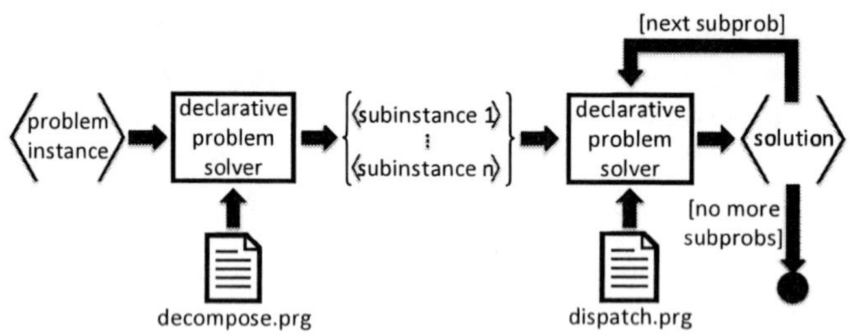

Fig. 2. Data flow of the scheduling process

Figure 2 shows the data flow of the scheduling process. First, the solver combines the instance with the decomposition program, that divides it into a number of subinstances. Both the number of subinstances and the decomposition strategy are determined by *decompose.prg*. Once the subinstances have been created, they are processed sequentially by the declarative solver following the dispatching rule defined in *dispatch.prg*. The dispatching process is incremental. Thus, the solution of one subinstance is forwarded as an additional input to the next subinstance in line until no more subinstances are left. The overall solution is the composition of all the subsolutions.

Prototype We build a prototype in order to provide a first proof of concept. Our prototype scheduler is implemented in Java incorporating ASCASS, a constraint answer set programming (CASP) solver [20]. ASCASS follows the idea given in [2], i.e. answer set programming (ASP) is used for specification of constraint satisfaction problems (CSPs). The CSPs are solved by the constraint solver Jacop. CASP approaches have proven to be highly effective for problems with very large domains, like industrial sized scheduling problems [3]. This is due to the

[3] http://www.gecode.org/
[4] http://jacop.osolpro.com/
[5] http://potassco.sourceforge.net/

combination of the high-level knowledge representation features of ASP and the possibility of stating the variable domains as intervals by means of constraint variables. Since the scheduling problems usually present large domains for the time representation, CASP suits well our needs.

In our prototype the decomposition strategy implemented in *decompose.prg* splits the input based on the predefined machine and workcenter information. This means that every subinstance only comprises a single machine of each workcenter. This makes sure that it is possible to process every operation type in every subinstance. In order to balance the workload, the set of jobs is equally divided among the subinstances. Concerning the dispatching rule, we apply the most-total-work-remaining (MTWR) rule. In our implementation, this rule is expressed as a logic predicate specifying the operation priorities in a recursive manner, i.e.

```
opPriority(J,L):-
  op(J), opLength(J,L), not precedes(J,_).
opPriority(J,P2+L):-
  op(J), op(J2), precedes(J,J2), opPriority(J2,P2), opLength(J,L).
```

The declarative solver (ASCASS) processes the operations conforming the stated priorities, behaving in accordance to the MTWR rule[6].

Example In the following we describe the behavior of our prototype on a small sample instance. Take the following FJSP instance, represented as logic facts:

```
machine(1).machine(2).machine(3).machine(4).
machineWorkcenter(1,1).machineWorkcenter(2,1).
machineWorkcenter(3,2).machineWorkcenter(4,2).
%job 1
op(11).opLength(11,2).opWorkcenter(11,2).precedes(11,12).
op(12).opLength(12,3).opWorkcenter(12,1).
%job 2
op(21).opLength(21,3).opWorkcenter(21,1).precedes(21,22).
op(22).opLength(22,2).opWorkcenter(22,2).precedes(22,23).
op(23).opLength(23,4).opWorkcenter(23,1).
%job 3
op(31).opLength(31,8).opWorkcenter(31,1).precedes(31,32).
op(32).opLength(32,2).opWorkcenter(32,2).
%job 4
op(41).opLength(41,2).opWorkcenter(41,1).precedes(41,42)
op(42).opLength(42,1).opWorkcenter(42,2).precedes(42,43).
op(43).opLength(43,7).opWorkcenter(43,1).
```

The above code snippet encodes:

- four machines organized in two workcenters

[6] For space reasons it is not possible to go further into the implementation details of the prototype. The interested reader can find further information on programming in ASCASS and our prototype at http://isbi.aau.at/HINT

- four jobs, whereby jobs 1 and 3 consist of two operations and job 2 and 4 consist of three operations, whereby
- every operation has a defined operation length, and the *precedes* predicate indicates the operation ordering within a job.

The decomposition method used in our prototype splits the sample input in two subinstances. Each of the subinstances comprises one machine per workcenter. The jobs are equally distributed among the subinstances, such that the first one contains jobs 1 and 2, and the second contains job 3 and 4.
For the first subinstance, the dispatch program produces the following operation

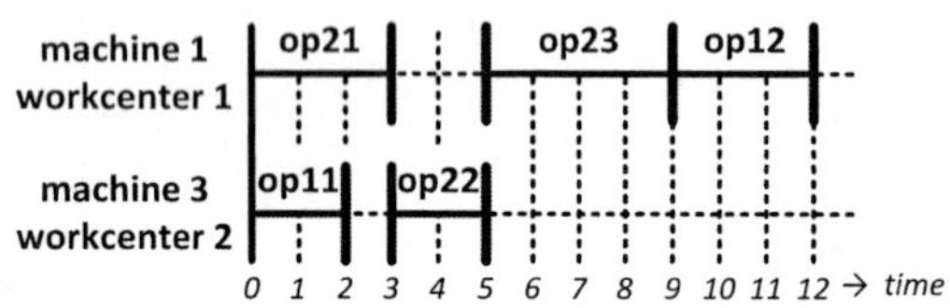

Fig. 3. Partial scheduling solution of the sample instance

priorities conforming to MTWR: op12=3, op11=5; op23=4, op22=6, op21=9. The operations are handled compliant with the priorities in descending order, i.e. highest priority operations first. Consequently, the partial solution in Figure 3 is produced. The overall solution is composed by this subsolution and the subsolution of the second subinstance.

3 Benchmark

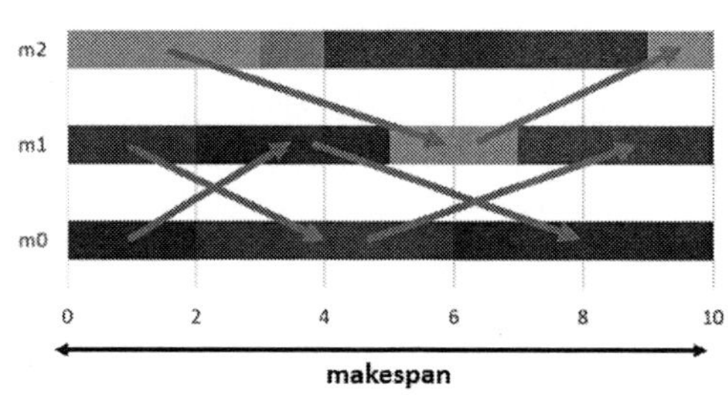

Fig. 4. Principle of instance generation

For evaluation purposes we produced test instances of realistic sizes which are on the one hand patterned on problems of our project partner Infineon

Austria Technologies and on the other hand have the advantage of proven minimal makespans. This is accomplished by first producing an optimal solution without machine idle times for a given number of operations (#ops) to be scheduled on a given number of machines (#machines) and the minimal makespan. This is done by randomly partitioning the machines' time continuum $[0..makespan \times \#machines - 1]$ into number of operations many partitions whereby each partition corresponds to the processing period of an operation. Consequently, the minimal makespan, average operation length (avg(opLength)), number of operations (#ops) and number of machines (#machines) relate conforming to $makespan = \frac{\#ops \times avg(opLength)}{\#machines}$. Based on such a partitioning, successor relations are randomly generated. Each operation gets at most one successor and/or predecessor such that the successor's starting time is greater than the predecessor's finishing time. Figure 4 shows the principle for 11 operations (5 jobs) on 3 machines and a minimal makespan of 10.

We applied two different procedures for generating random successor relations based on the pre-calculated solution:

1. For each operation *op* (in random order) define as successor *suc* a random operation such that
   - *suc* is not on the same machine as *op*.
   - *suc* starts later than *op* ends.
   - *suc* is not yet a successor of another operation.
   - If no such *suc* exists *op* has no successor.
2. For each operation *op* (in random order) define as successor *suc* an operation such that
   - *suc* is not on the same machine as *op*.
   - *suc* starts later than *op* ends.
   - *suc* is not yet a successor of another operation and
   - the time between *op* ends and *suc* starts is minimal.
   - In case that there are multiple possible successors, a random one is chosen.
   - If no such *suc* exists *op* has no successor.

The two different generating approaches result in benchmark instances which are different in nature: (1) produces many jobs consisting of a small number of operations. We refer to this set of instances as 'short-jobs' (SJ). On the contrary, (2) produces fewer jobs but with a larger number of operations per job. We refer to this set of instances as 'long-jobs' (LJ). For each machine/operations setting, i.e. 10 machines / 100 operations, 10 machines / 1000 operations, 100 machines / 1000 operations and 100 machines / 10000 operations we produced three basic instances (files). Each of the basic instances stands for a set of instances, depending whether the instance is interpreted as JSP or FJSP and which flexibility factor is assumed in the FJSP. A flexibility of 1 stands for the JSP, i.e. all machines are different to each other. A flexibility of 2 means that each operation can be processed by two machines, i.e. there is always two machines of the same type. For 10 machines we produced instances for the flexibility factors 1 (i.e. the

JSP), 2, 5 and 10 (i.e. all machines can process all operations). For 100 machines we produced instances for the flexibility factors 1, 2, 5, 10, 20, 50 and 100. This results in 66 instances for the long-jobs benchmark and the same number of instances for the short-jobs benchmark. All instances have a minimal makespan of 600000, which, interpreted in seconds, constitutes roughly one week. Tables 1 and 2 show the statistics for the benchmark. The whole benchmark is available online at http://isbi.aau.at/hint/scheduling-prototype.

	#machines/#ops	file	numJobs	minNumOps	maxNumOps	avgNumOps
LJ	10/100	1	12	4	12	8.3
LJ	10/100	2	14	3	13	7.1
LJ	10/100	3	14	4	11	7.1
LJ	10/1000	1	18	10	75	55.6
LJ	10/1000	2	18	1	79	55.6
LJ	10/1000	3	17	2	83	58.8
LJ	100/1000	1	102	2	16	9.8
LJ	100/1000	2	103	4	16	9.7
LJ	100/1000	3	102	2	17	9.8
LJ	100/10000	1	102	68	134	98.0
LJ	100/10000	2	103	71	122	97.1
LJ	100/10000	3	103	5	133	97.1
SJ	10/100	1	32	1	5	3.1
SJ	10/100	2	33	1	5	3
SJ	10/100	3	32	1	7	3.1
SJ	10/1000	1	245	2	11	4.1
SJ	10/1000	2	232	1	9	4.3
SJ	10/1000	3	236	2	10	4.2
SJ	100/1000	1	285	1	8	3.5
SJ	100/1000	2	285	1	8	3.5
SJ	100/1000	3	286	1	7	3.5
SJ	100/10000	1	2174	2	15	4.6
SJ	100/10000	2	2153	2	13	4.6
SJ	100/10000	3	2161	2	14	4.6

Table 1. Benchmark statistics: operations per job

4 Experiment

The main goal of our experiment is to provide a first proof of concept of our novel scheduling approach. In particular, we want to investigate the impact of problem decomposition on our large-scale scheduling benchmark. The purpose of this experiment is not to investigate the performance of different dispatching rules. Instead, we want to show that dispatching rules in general can be successfully exploited in the context of declarative programming and problem decomposition.

4.1 Setup

We tested our prototype described in Section 2 against the benchmark instances described in Section 3. All the instances are solved once with the decomposition approach, also described in Section 2, and once without decomposition. In both cases, we use the most total work remaining (MTWR) dispatching rule. The

	#machines/#ops	file	minOpLength	maxOpLength	avgOpLength
LJ	10/100	1	109	306357	60000
LJ	10/100	2	187	369450	60000
LJ	10/100	3	105	338068	60000
LJ	10/1000	1	11	41650	6000
LJ	10/1000	2	2	57111	6000
LJ	10/1000	3	8	45096	6000
LJ	100/1000	1	48	558806	60000
LJ	100/1000	2	144	464127	60000
LJ	100/1000	3	15	432530	60000
LJ	100/10000	1	2	54454	6000
LJ	100/10000	2	1	64436	6000
LJ	100/10000	3	2	59748	6000
SJ	10/100	1	52	403461	60000
SJ	10/100	2	1951	307065	60000
SJ	10/100	3	414	249757	60000
SJ	10/1000	1	4	46271	6000
SJ	10/1000	2	20	39801	6000
SJ	10/1000	3	9	54007	6000
SJ	100/1000	1	61	484415	60000
SJ	100/1000	2	116	384096	60000
SJ	100/1000	3	3	531413	60000
SJ	100/10000	1	1	64636	6000
SJ	100/10000	2	1	52669	6000
SJ	100/10000	3	1	59361	6000

Table 2. Benchmark statistics: operation lengths

experiment was conducted on a system with Intel i7-3930K CPU (3.20GHz), 64 Gb of RAM. The timeout for the computation of the complete schedule for each instance was set to 4000 seconds. This time frame would allow a frequent recalculation in a weekly or bi-weekly scheduling scenario.

4.2 Results

	#mach/#ops	JSP	FJSP-2	FJSP-5	FJSP-10	FJSP-20	FJSP-50	FJSP-100	total
no dec	10/100	100%	100%	100%	0%	-	-	-	75%
dec	10/100	100%	100%	100%	100%	-	-	-	100%
no dec	10/1000	100%	100%	0%	0%	-	-	-	50%
dec	10/1000	100%	100%	100%	100%	-	-	-	100%
no dec	100/1000	100%	100%	66.7%	0%	0%	0%	0%	38%
dec	100/1000	100%	100%	100%	100%	100%	100%	100%	100%
no dec	100/10000	83.3%	0%	0%	0%	0%	0%	0%	11.9%
dec	100/10000	83.3%	100%	100%	100%	100%	100%	100%	97.6%
no dec	total	95.8%	75%	58.4%	0%	0%	0%	0%	38.6%
dec	total	95.8%	100%	100%	100%	100%	100%	100%	99.2%

Table 3. Comparison of percentage of solved instances of the approaches with and without decomposition

Table 3 shows the percentage of solved instances for the different machines/operation settings. The first column distinguishes between the approaches with decomposition (dec) and without decomposition (no dec). The results are given grouped by the different flexibility factors, i.e. the number of possible machines for each operation. It gets obvious that the sizes of the job-shop in terms of number of machines/operations as a big impact in the number of solved instances. In particular, less instances can be solved without producing a timeout in larger job-shops. On the other hand, also the increase of the flexibility factor negatively impacts on the number of solved instances. A particular result is the case with flexibility of 5, where in the approach without decomposition it was possible to solve 66.7% of the 100/1000 instances, but 0% of the 10/1000 instances. The reason behind this behavior is the ratio between the number of operations and the number of machines. In the case with 100 machines and 1000 operations the ratio is 10, meaning that in a perfectly balanced schedule, where all the machines get the same amount of operations, there are 10 operations per machine. In the case of 10 machines and 1000 operations the ratio is 100 operations per machine. An increased number of operations per machine leads to a longer constraint propagation in the general declarative problem solver.

Concerning the instances with 10 machines and 1000 operations, 12 out of 24 (50%) were solved. In the set of instances with 100 machines and 1000 operations, the number of solved instances was 16 out of 42 (38%). Note, the varying number of total instances (24 vs. 42) is due to the varying number of machines in the different settings. A greater number of machines naturally allows more flexibility factors. The total number of solved instances of the approach without decomposition is 51 out of 132, which corresponds to 38.6% of the benchmark.

In comparison, the decomposition approach showed better results. With respect to the JSP, the results are the same as in the approach without decomposition, because the JSP corresponds to a FJSP with flexibility of 1. Consequently, no decomposition occurs, as the workcenters cannot be split any further. In all the other cases the decomposition plays a crucial role in the solvability, since it was possible to solve all the FJSP instances with any size of the problem. The only unsolved case is a JSP instance with 100 machines and 10000 operations, where the decomposition is not applied. Overall it was possible to solve 131 out of 132 (99.2%) instances, proving the effectiveness of the decomposition approach. Table 4 shows the makespans produced by MTWR without decomposition (no dec) and with decomposition (dec) respectively. The term *t/o* indicates where the instances reached the timeout. It is to be noticed that, when it is possible to find a solution, the approach without decomposition presents a lower makespan.

	#mach/#ops	**JSP**	**FJSP-2**	**FJSP-5**	**FJSP-10**	**FJSP-20**	**FJSP-50**	**FJSP-100**
no dec	10/100	855350	712685	645226	t/o	-	-	-
dec	10/100	855350	1067370	1093303	1014521	-	-	-
no dec	10/1000	780589	696931	t/o	t/o	-	-	-
dec	10/1000	780589	995531	1083530	995953	-	-	-
no dec	100/1000	933775	754580	670931	t/o	t/o	t/o	t/o
dec	100/1000	933775	1170844	1426045	1451335	1686282	1418501	1193235
no dec	100/10000	767278	t/o	t/o	t/o	t/o	t/o	t/o
dec	100/10000	767278	1035810	1225529	1295864	1353059	1365883	1236629

Table 4. Comparison of the makespan results (in seconds) of the two approaches

This is due to the fact that the decomposition program used in our experiment aims to distribute the job equally among the subinstances. However, the number of operations per job varies in the benchmark. Thus, an equal number of jobs in the subinstances does not necessarily correspond to an equal number of operations. Consequently, the total workload to be processed in the subinstances is not perfectly balanced. Opportune tuning of the decomposition program may lead to better results in terms of makespan. This will be investigated in future work.

	#mach/#ops	JSP	FJSP-2	FJSP-5	FJSP-10	FJSP-20	FJSP-50	FJSP-100
no dec	10/100	0.1	0.1	2.1	t/o	-	-	-
dec	10/100	0.1	0.2	0.2	0.2	-	-	-
no dec	10/1000	86.3	436	t/o	t/o	-	-	-
dec	10/1000	86.3	91.6	76.0	57.1	-	-	-
no dec	100/1000	1.3	2.1	839.5	t/o	t/o	t/o	t/o
dec	100/1000	1.3	1.1	0.9	0.9	0.9	0.9	0.9
no dec	100/10000	2611.8	t/o	t/o	t/o	t/o	t/o	t/o
dec	100/10000	2611.8	2963	1970.5	1516.5	1133.7	1130.7	449

Table 5. Comparison of the runtime results (in seconds) of the two approaches

Finally, Table 5 shows the actual runtimes for solution calculations without decomposition (no dec) and with decomposition (dec) respectively. The decomposition approach was capable to solve the instances significantly quicker than without decomposition.

5 Conclusion

We presented a novel scheduling approach targeted to large job-shop and flexible job-shop problems. The approach combines the high level knowledge representation of declarative programming with problem decomposition and dispatching rules. We introduced a new large-scale scheduling benchmark of instances comprising up to 10000 job operations to be scheduled on up to 100 machines and with proven optimal solutions. We provided a first evaluation for a prototype implementation of our approach. The results clearly prove the concept of our scheduling method. In particular, with this method it was possible to find schedules for all the large-scale instances of the benchmark before a predefined timeout occured, while without decomposition, many instances could not be solved. Summarizing, we can conclude that the combination of declarative methods, problem decomposition and dispatching rules can successfully be applied in real-world large-scale scheduling domains.

References

1. Azi, N., Gendreau, M., Potvin, J.Y.: A dynamic vehicle routing problem with multiple delivery routes. Annals of Operations Research 199(1), 103–112 (2012)

2. Balduccini, M.: Representing constraint satisfaction problems in answer set programming. In: ICLP09 Workshop on Answer Set Programming and Other Computing Paradigms (ASPOCP'09) (2009)
3. Balduccini, M.: Logic Programming and Nonmonotonic Reasoning: 11th International Conference, LPNMR 2011, Vancouver, Canada, May 16-19, 2011. Proceedings, chap. Industrial-Size Scheduling with ASP+CP, pp. 284–296. Springer Berlin Heidelberg (2011)
4. Bellman, R.: Mathematical aspects of scheduling theory. SIAM Jour of App Math 4, 168–205 (1956)
5. Bent, R., Van Hentenryck, P.: Spatial, temporal, and hybrid decompositions for large-scale vehicle routing with time windows. In: Cohen, D. (ed.) Proceedings of the 16th International Conference on Principles and Practice of Constraint Programming (CP 2010). pp. 99–113. Springer Berlin Heidelberg, Berlin, Heidelberg (2010)
6. Blazewicz, J., Ecker, K., Pesch, E., Schmidt, G., Weglarz, J.: Handbook on Scheduling: Models and Methods for Advanced Planning (International Handbooks on Information Systems). Springer-Verlag New York, Inc., Secaucus, NJ, USA (2007)
7. Carchrae, T., Beck, J.C.: Principles for the design of large neighborhood search. Journal of Mathematical Modelling and Algorithms 8(3), 245–270 (2009)
8. Demirkol, E., Mehta, S., Uzsoy, R.: Benchmarks for shop scheduling problems. European Journal of Operational Research 109(1), 137 – 141 (1998), http://www.sciencedirect.com/science/article/pii/S0377221797000192
9. Easton, T., Singireddy, A.: A large neighborhood search heuristic for the longest common subsequence problem. Journal of Heuristics 14(3), 271–283 (2008)
10. Fogliatto, F.S., Da Silveira, G.J.C., Borenstein, D.: The mass customization decade: An updated review of the literature. International Journal of Production Economics 138(1), 14–25 (2012)
11. Garey, M.R.: The complexity of flowshop and jobshop scheduling. Mathematics of Operations Research 1(2), 117–129 (1976)
12. Garey, M.R., Johnson, D.S.: Computers and Intractability. A Guide to the Theory of NP-Completeness. W. H. Freeman and Company (1979)
13. Gebser, M., Kaminski, R., Kaufmann, B., Schaub, T.: Answer Set Solving in Practice. Synthesis Lectures on Artificial Intelligence and Machine Learning, Morgan and Claypool Publishers (2012)
14. Gebser, M., Ostrowski, M., Schaub, T.: Constraint Answer Set Solving, pp. 235–249. Springer Berlin Heidelberg, Berlin, Heidelberg (2009)
15. Hildebrandt, T., Goswami, D., Freitag, M.: Large-scale simulation-based optimization of semiconductor dispatching rules. In: Proceedings of the 2014 Winter Simulation Conference. pp. 2580–2590. WSC '14, IEEE Press, Piscataway, NJ, USA (2014), http://dl.acm.org/citation.cfm?id=2693848.2694175
16. Holweg, M.: The genealogy of lean production. Journal of Operations Management 25(2), 420–437 (2007), special Issue Evolution of the Field of Operations Management SI/ Special Issue Organisation Theory and Supply Chain Management
17. Hurink, J., Jurisch, B., Thole, M.: Tabu search for the job-shop scheduling problem with multi-purpose machines. Operations-Research-Spektrum 15(4), 205–215 (1994)
18. Kaban, A.K., Othman, Z., Rohmah, D.S.: Comparison of dispatching rules in job-shop scheduling problem using simulation: a case study. International Journal of Simulation Modelling 11(3), 129–140 (2012)

19. Pacino, D., Van Hentenryck, P.: Large neighborhood search and adaptive randomized decompositions for flexible jobshop scheduling. International Joint Conference on Artificial Intelligence. Proceedings (2011)
20. Teppan, E.C., Friedrich, G.: Heuristic constraint answer set programming. In: Proceedings of the 6th International Workshop on Combinations of Intelligent Methods and Applications (CIMA16 at ECAI16) (2016)

Scheduling Regarding Energy Efficiency

Jürgen Sauer

University of Oldenburg
Department of Computer Science
D-26111 Oldenburg
juergen.sauer@uni-oldenburg.de

Abstract Reducing energy consumption is one of the actual challenges in all parts of industry. This can lead to a low carbon footprint for activities under consideration as well as to cost effective reductions of overall energy consumptions. This paper shows how intelligent scheduling strategies can be used to limit energy consumption in production to a given range. Especially the "right" scheduling of energy intensive production processes can lead to a reduction of overall or peak energy needs and this also has some advantages regarding costs.

Introduction

Nearly all areas of production and logistics have presented their own „we are going green" proposals. Most often green means the reduction of carbon dioxide mainly by lower power consumption but also reducing waste or dangerous ingredients etc. can be found as goals to meet. Several actions may be taken to achieve these goals:

- using new technologies e.g. in the production process may reduce ingredients, waste as well as energy consumption
- using new machines may reduce energy consumption and waste
- changing ingredients may reduce energy consumption
- rescheduling the production process may reduce energy consumption.

The last topic is tackled in this paper. Especially the "right" scheduling of energy intensive production processes can lead to a reduction of overall or peak energy needs and this also has some advantages regarding costs.

The costs of energy consumption typically are based on several components [1]. The two most important are shown in figure 1. One is the overall consumption of energy during a given time period, most often this is one year. The "Arbeitspreis" is calculated using Euros per KiloWattHours (kWh), actually around 0,10 Euro. Another important component is the payment for peak energy demands. These peaks define the maximum power needed during the time period. Typically the peak demand and the power usage are measured every 15 minutes. Only a few peaks, sometimes only one, are then used for the calculation of the peak consumption costs. The peak consumption results in a "Leistungspreis" which is calculated using the peak demand in kW and has an actual price around 45 Euros per kW. E.g. if we have a company that uses 2500 Mio. kWh per year and has a peak demand of 500000 kW this results in costs of 2.5 Mio. Euros for the consumption and 22.445 Mio. Euros for the peak. So the reduction of peaks can have enormous effects on the energy costs.

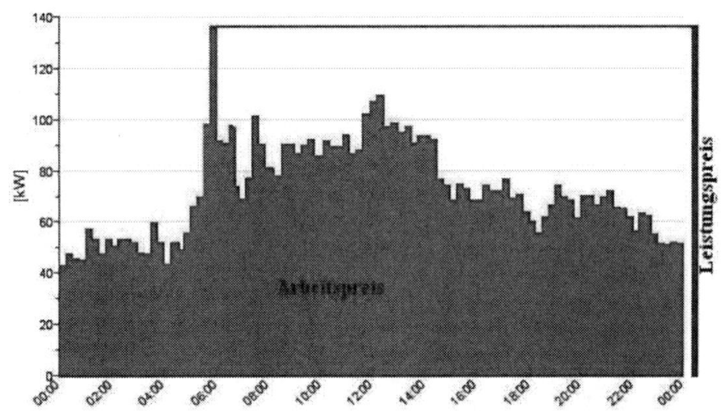

Fig. 1. Components of the energy cost calculation [2]

But also the energy provider can benefit from the peak demand reduction. Typically, the consumer makes a forecast and announcement of his peak energy needs. With this forecasts the energy provider plans its energy production. And it has to plan for all possible peaks even if the energy is not used. This is necessary because if the peaks are exceeded, the whole power provisioning is endangered. This can easily occur if machines are used in parallel and several of the energy peaks of the production processes will superimpose. Therefore most of the companies have some kind of emergency plan when the energy consumption approaches the upper bounds, e.g. the immediate shut down of machines. But this is disturbing the whole manufacturing process and eventually damaging the machines. This is another reason for looking for a scheduling solution that can lead to a production schedule that avoids the power consumption peaks.

The production of plastic parts using the injection molding process is a good example and will be described in the following section and used throughout the paper.

This paper is part of the actual project "Scheduling4Green" and will present at first some of the problems and production processes in which the scheduling according to energy consumption will lead to main advantages. This is followed by some ideas and approaches on how to cope with the scheduling regarding energy consumption. An example from injection molding is used to illustrate the problems and approaches.

The problem: efficient energy use in production

Most of the production processes are using special equipment within the single steps that are performed. This equipment, typically machines or apparatus, needs energy on a constant basis or on a fluctuating basis. The fluctuation is generated by the energy consumption within the production process. Such fluctuation is found e.g. in most of the processes in which material has to be heated.

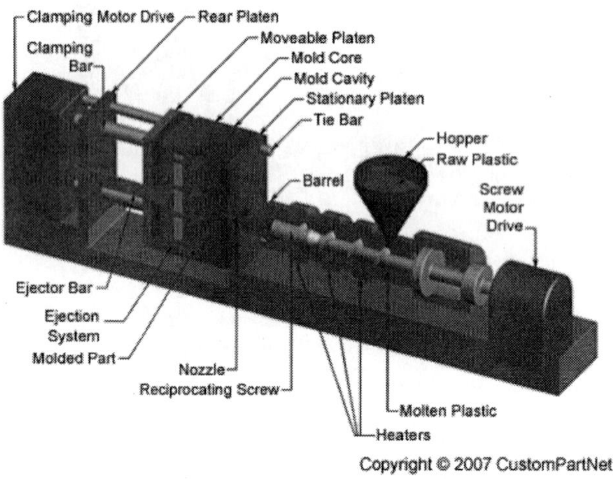

Fig. 2. Example of an Injection Molding Machine [3]

One example for such processes is injection molding. This technology is used for the production of a lot of products and parts mostly made up of plastics. Figure 2 shows an injection molding machine in which typically the following process steps [3, 4] are performed:

1. Granulated plastic is filled in the hopper and the mold closes
2. The granulated plastic is heated to fluid polymer
3. The fluid polymer is injected into the mold cavity
4. The cave is pressed and the pressure on the cave is maintained for a specific time
5. The part is cooled down
6. The part is ejected from the mold.

Power demand is a combination of several factors, main parts are heating and pressure [5]. Figure 3 shows an example of two power consumption profiles of such a process [6]. The difference in the power consumption of the process steps is one of the problems we have to cope with.

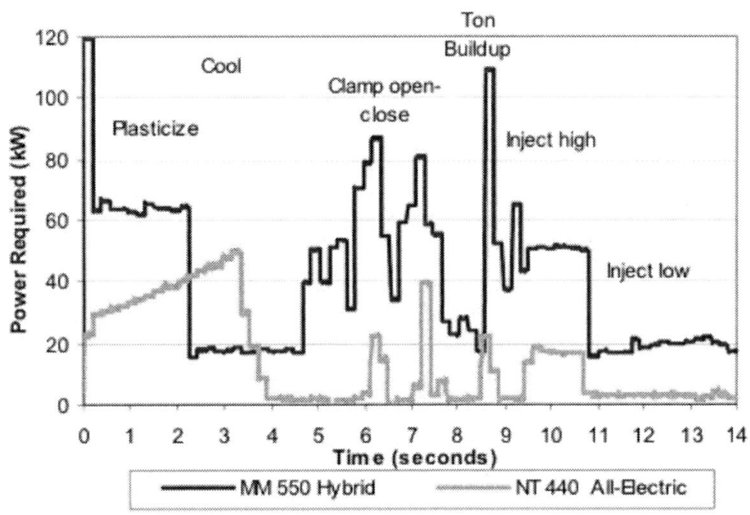

Fig. 3. Examples of Energy Profiles of Injection Molding Machines [6]

To show the effects on the energy usage we use several scenarios that are adopted from a project partner from the injection molding industry (http://www.ostendorf-kunststoffe.com) [7]. In a first scenario we investigate a case with more than one but nearly identical machines. The scenario contains five machines that are able to produce two different products but every machine has its own energy demand profiles for each of the products. Table 1 shows the duration (in seconds) and the energy demand (in kW) for each of the process steps mentioned before for the first product.

Table 1. Process Times and Energy Demand for Product A

Phase/ Machine	M1	M2	M3	M4	M5
0.Prepare	5/0	7/0	4/0	5/0	2/0
1.Close	1/150	1/150	2/75	1/160	1/180
2.Heat	4/50	3/60	3/60	6/40	5/65
3.Inject	1/150	1/165	2/130	1/150	1/180
4.Pressure	3/120	2/130	2/150	2/130	3/100
5.Cool	9/100	7/140	6/110	9/100	6/105
6.Eject	2/75	2/85	3/80	4/65	3/75

With this information we can show the energy profiles of each of the machines and also can investigate the effects of energy usage if all machines are working. Figure 4 shows the energy profiles of the five machines for product A and figure 5 the single profiles as well as the accumulated energy profile (*Sum*) if all machines have their peak demand at the same time.

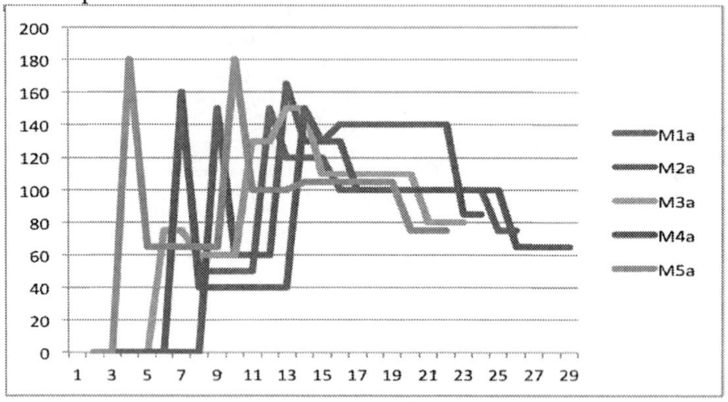

Fig. 4. Energy Profiles of Machines for Product A

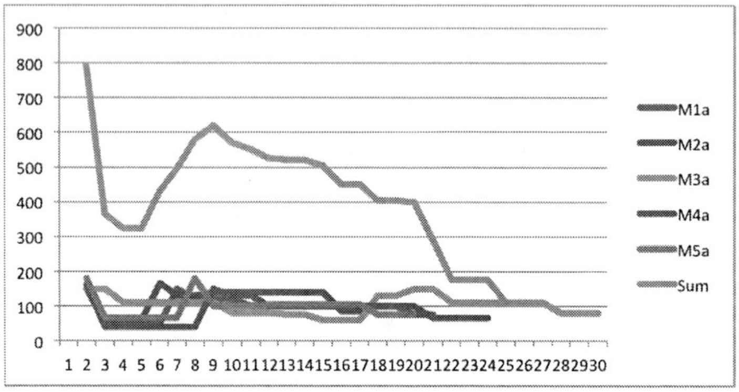

Fig. 5. Energy Profile with all Peaks at the same Time

So the main challenge will be to produce a schedule that will avoid such peaks created by unfavorable overlays. A simple shift of the production is not sufficient because this does not guarantee the avoiding of parallel peaks. Additionally, this will extend the production and delivery times (measured by makespan), which also may be an important feature. Thus the next section will describe possible approaches to avoid energy demand peaks but also tries to keep makespan as low as possible or to keep due dates.

Concept of a scheduling system regarding energy usage

As stated in the section before the main goal of a scheduling algorithm that regards the energy consumption should be to keep the energy needs in a given range and to avoid peaks. But also other goals are to be regarded e.g. makespan of the production. Therefore we developed a concept and a system that allows us to test the effects of different scheduling strategies to the injection molding problem [8, 9, 10].

The concept consists of two main components. One component is a simulation model of the injection molding scenario. This is used to get an impression of the production process as well as to test the schedules that are result of the different strategies under investigation. It also offers the possibility to gather data during the simulated production process and then to plot some of the resulting data, e.g. the energy usage over time.

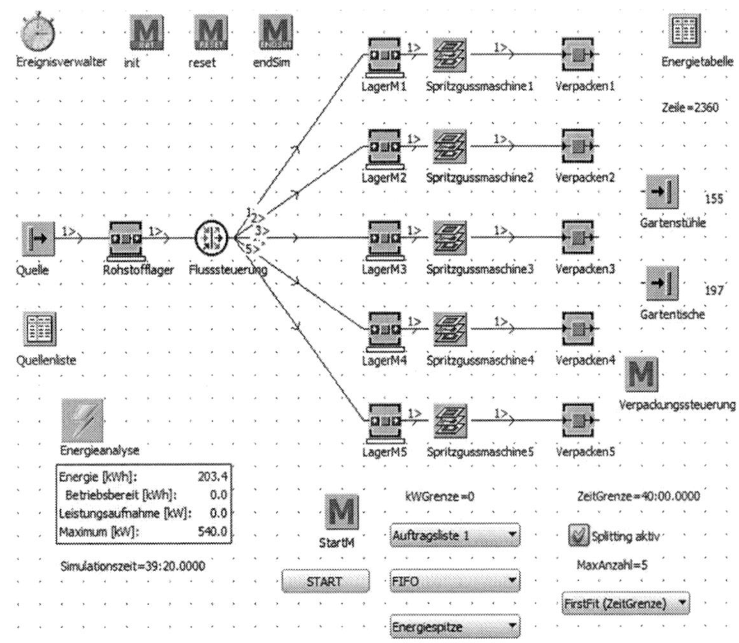

Fig. 6. PlantSimulation Model of Injection Molding Scenario

Figure 6 gives a sketch of the model build with PlantSimulation. Each machine (Spritzgussmaschine*x*) is modelled in more detail by an own network showing the single production steps to be performed including the energy consumption during the steps. During the simulation the energy consumption is collected and can be plotted after the simulation process.

The second component of the approach is the scheduling component. It is intended to allow the test of several different scheduling strategies. It consists of modular scheduling algorithms that can be configured by the user and calculate schedules that can be simulated with the simulation component.

The different strategies that will be investigated during the project are:

- Shifting production processes
  this only works for identical machines with identical energy profile, otherwise it can not be guaranteed that peaks are avoided and typically makespan is extended.
- Use an approximation and heuristics
  this is described in the following
- Use improvement strategies
  this is actual and further work, e.g. use simulated annealing approach to improve both energy reduction as well as makespan or meeting the due dates.

To find adequate heuristics one can look for related work in the area. There are only few publications regarding the topic of peak power reduction. In [11] a "lazy algorithm" for a two task problem in energy provision of buildings is presented that uses control states of the tasks two switch between these. The heuristic is problem specific and the approach does not allow the test of different strategies. In anorher project we have investigated a problem from the area of glas production [12].

The approach we use bases on the following design decisions:

1. Use a simpler form of energy profile
2. Find an appropriate problem representation and use general heuristics for that problem in combination with problem specific heuristics.

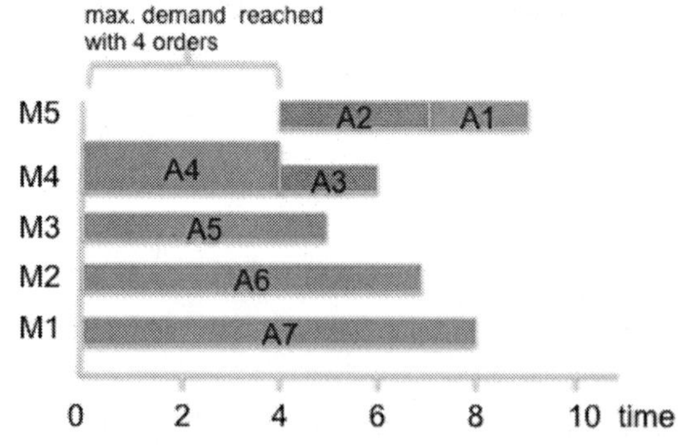

Fig. 7. Example of a Schedule with Energy Demand Information

The first design decision leads to a representation of the energy profile with a rectangular function. This is feasible because the production processes are quite short. Therefore a schedule then looks like shown in figure 7. The bars show the length of the operation and the capacity (energy) needed according to the simplified profile. The example in figure 7 then shows immediately that the upper bound of energy usage is reached with only four orders during the first four time units. Additionally, we do not try to minimize energy consumption, because this can lead to a schedule where only one machine at a time is used. Instead we introduce an upper bound for energy usage that should not be extended and also allows a timely finishing of orders. The scheduling problem then has some similarity with a bin packing problem. Thus we adopt the model and heuristics from bin packing [13] and can formulate the problem as follows:

> Given a set of orders and machines that can perform the orders and an energy usage limit, find a schedule (an assignment of orders to machines) with:
> - All orders are scheduled
> - The limit of energy usage is not extended at any time (which can be compared to: the number of bins is minimal).

Thus the machines are seen as the bins that can be filled with orders up to a given time limit. The number of machines in parallel determines the energy usage and therefore this number shall be as low as possible.

Several heuristic strategies have been presented to solve the bin packing problem [13]. To find a minimum number of bins the *first fit strategy* is used most often. It says that the first possible bin is used that does not extend its capacity. Here it means that the first possible machine can be used if the start is possible and the energy bound is not extended. Otherwise a time shift is necessary.

To use the bins evenly the *worst case strategy* has been proposed. Here the bin is selected that leaves the most space for other objects. This is selected in order to find a schedule with a minimal duration which also provides a good energy usage.

As the strategies have been formulated for different goals they will lead to different results also in the injection molding case.

The selected strategies are integrated with some problem specific heuristics that have been successfully used in scheduling. These heuristics combine a general problem decomposition heuristic (*order based scheduling* [14]) with some specific heuristics for the selection of the next order to be processed respectively the next machine to be checked. Together these lead to the following basic algorithm:

```
1: init orderlist; init machinelist; init plan;
2: while orderlist /= empty
3:   order:- orderselection(orderlist)
4:   machine:- machineselection(plan, order, machinelist)
5:   plan:- updateplan(plan, machine, order)
6:   update orderlist; update machinelist;
7: end while
```

Within the algorithm several degrees of freedom are incorporated that lead to a huge amount of possible strategies that can be implemented. For the *orderselection* several rules are possible, e.g. FIFO, LIFO, shortest operation time, longest operation time and a combination of product and operation time. The *machineselection* contains the overall strategy from bin packing (first fit resp. worst fit) as well as some rules for selecting the next machine from a given machine list, i.e. which machine to use next in the overall strategy. Here are rules like FIFO (by number), select by energy usage (lowest first) or by duration (shortest processing first) possible. Together this combination of basic algorithm with *first fit* and *worst fit strategy* and the other selection rules leads to a huge variety of algorithms that can be selected by the user and tested for their quality. Some results are shown in the next section.

Implementation and first results

The concept presented in the previous section was implemented using the PlantSimulation Software [15]. The model of the injection process has already been presented in figure 6. The basic algorithm together with the selection processes have been implemented using the SimTalk language of the PlantSimulation framework [10]. The user can select the combination of rules and the PlantSimulation system will plot some results after the simulation.

The test scenario consists of five machines with different power demand functions for each of the two products, two products that can be produced on either of the machines, four order sets for production to stock which are representative for different order configurations (mixed, only one product, huge amounts), the basic algorithm as described above with the two strategies and the selection rules.

All combinations of resulting algorithms have been tested with all four order sets. Additionally, a splitting of orders has also been implemented.

Table 2 shows some overall results for the first set of orders (22 orders for the two different products with different amounts of the products) with the best cases from the different test configurations. Within the two strategies particular combinations of selection heuristic lead to better results than others. Within the first fit strategy the combination of "select order by product name" and "select machine by shortest processing time" leads in most cases to the best results. In the worst case strategy no rule combination outperforms the others.

Table 2. First results

Case	Given Energy Limit	Given Time Limit	Energy Peak	Duration
Random PlantSim	-	-	830	28:00.0000
FirstFit	400	-	380	50:06.0000
FirstFit	600	-	590	34:48.0000
FirstFit	800	-	745	27:00.0000
WorstFit	-	30:00.0000	640	30:00.0000
WorstFit	-	50:00.0000	475	49:53.0000

As expected low energy usage leads to less machines but longer times, short times (makespan) leads to higher energy peaks. Figure 8 shows the diagrams of the energy consumption during the simulation process for the 800 kW bounded solution (below) compared with the randomly generated solution by PlantSimulation (above). It shows that the energy usage is more evenly distributed, does not extend the given upper bound and is even shorter than the random solution.

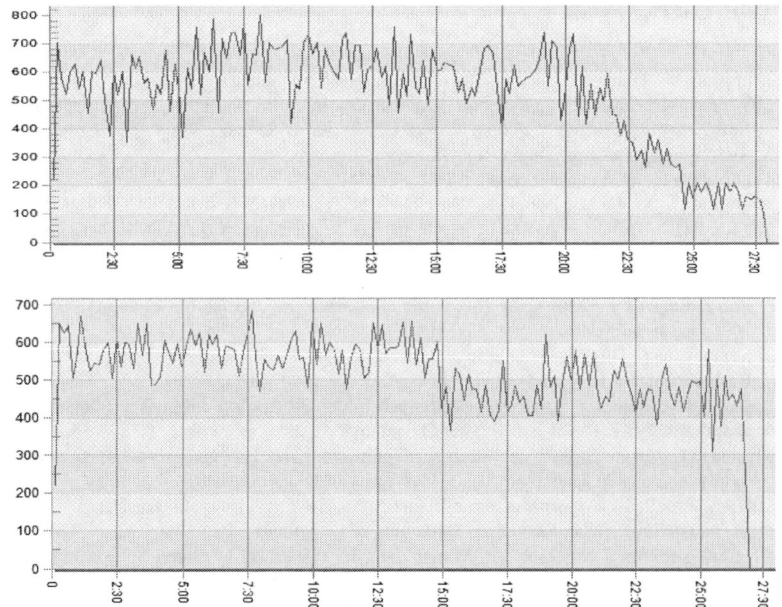

Fig. 8. Energy Consumption of Random and Bounded Solutions

Conclusion and further work

The paper presents a solution for the problem of finding schedules for a injection molding production that do not exceed a given peak energy usage and that try to keep the makespan of the schedules as low as possible. The approach bases on the approximation of the problem by a bin packing problem and the use of adequate heuristics. The results show, that it is possible to schedule with given upper bounds of energy usage. In the first strategies implemented the fulfilment of both goals together is not in the focus and therefore is not as good as it might be. The actual work looks for some extension to improve both energy usage and makespan or due dates. Here we investigate iterative improvement strategies like simulated annealing that can be used in the search for solutions that obey multi-objectives [16]. Additionally, the problem scenario presented here uses a five machine model that has some restrictions that are not realistic, e.g. lead times are to short, all machines can produce all products. Thus the model will be extended to be more realistic.

References

[1] https://www.transnetbw.de/de/netzzugang/entgelt/berechnung

[2] Wilken, M.: Entwicklung eines Systems zur Optimierung der Energieeffizienz in der Kunststoffspritzgussindustrie, Diploma Thesis, Universität Oldenburg, 2008.

[3] www.xcentricmold.com/about-injection-molding.php

[4] http://www.custompartnet.com/wu/InjectionMolding

[5] Madan, J., Mani, M., Lyons, K.W.: CHARACTERIZING ENERGY CONSUMPTION OF THE INJECTION MOLDING PROCESS, in: Proceedings of the ASME 2013 International Manufacturing Science and Engineering Conference MSEC2013, 2013.

[6] Thiriez, A., Gutowski, T.: An Environmental Analysis of Injection Molding, in: ISEE 2006, Proceedings of the 2006 IEEE International Symposium on Electronics and the Environment, 2006, pp. 195-200

[7] Simm, C., Wigbers, T.: Scheduling4Green unter Berücksichtigung reaktiver Planungsaspekte, Bachelor Thesis, University of Oldenburg, 2014.

[8] Giza, N.: Simulation von Energieverbrauch in der Produktion am Beispiel der Spritzgussindustrie, Bachelor Thesis, Universität Oldenburg, 2012.

[9] Kuhl, M.: Vergleich von Verfahren zur Optimierung des Energieverbrauchs in ausgewählten Industriebereichen, Bachelor Thesis, University of Oldenburg, 2014.

[10] Preuß, F.: Algorithmen zur Planung des Energieverbrauchs am Beispiel der Spritzgussherstellung, Bachelor Thesis, University of Oldenburg, 2015.

[11] Nghiem, T.X., Behl, M., Mangharam, R. Pappas, G.J.: Green Scheduling of Control Systems for Peak Demand Reduction, in: 50th IEEE Conference on Decision and Control and European Control Conference (CDC-ECC), Orlando, 2011, pp. 5131-5136

[12] Sauer, J., Runge, S.A., Bender, T.: Lastgangbezogene Prioritätsregeln für eine Produktionsplanung bei der Veredelung von Glasprodukten, in: J. Marx Gómez et al. (Eds.), IT-gestütztes Ressourcen- und Energiemanagement, Springer-Verlag, Berlin Heidelberg, 2013, pp. 3-9.

[13] Rager, M.: Energieorientierte Produktionsplanung, Gabler Edition Wissenschaft, 2006.

[14] Sauer, J.: Intelligente Ablaufplanung in lokalen und verteilten Anwendungsszenarien, Teubner, 2004.

[15] http://www.plm.automation.siemens.com/de_de/products/tecnomatix/plant_design/plant_simulation.shtml

[16] Dählmann, K.: Bewertung multikriterieller Produktionspläne zur energieeffizienten Maschinenbelegung in der Kunststoffproduktion, Master Thesis, University of Oldenburg, 2015.

AUTHOR INDEX

Da Col, Giacomo 34
Demberg, Vera 1
Drabble, Brian 27
Hoffmann, Jorg 1
Howcroft, David 1
Sauer, Jürgen 48
Schattenberg, Bernd 27
Schwenger, Maximilian 1
Teppan, Erich C. 34
Torralba, Alvaro 1